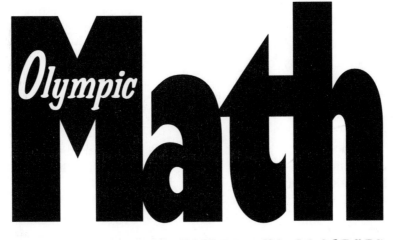

Olympic Math

GOLD MEDAL ACTIVITIES AND PROJECTS FOR GRADES 4-8

Sharon Vogt

GoodYearBooks

An Imprint of ScottForesman
A Division of HarperCollinsPublishers

Dedication

To my Mom, who earns two gold medals—one as a sports fan and the other as a mother. GoodYearBooks are available for most basic curriculum subjects plus many enrichment areas. For more GoodYearBooks, contact your local bookseller or educational dealer. For a complete catalog with information about other GoodYearBooks, please write:

GoodYearBooks
ScottForesman
1900 East Lake Avenue
Glenview, IL 60025

Illustrations by Douglas Klauba.

Book design by Patricia Lenihan-Barbee.

ISBN 0-673-36306-6

3 4 5 6 7 8 9 -DR- 03 02 01 00 99 98 97 96

Photo Credits

Unless otherwise acknowledged, all photographs are the property of Scott Foresman and Company. Page abbreviations are as follows: (t) top, (c) center, (b) bottom, (r) right, (l) left.

Front cover:
(tl)   UPI/Corbis-Bettmann
(tr)   UPI/Corbis-Bettmann
(bl)   UPI/Corbis-Bettmann
(br)   UPI/Corbis-Bettmann

Back cover:
(t)   UPI/Corbis-Bettmann
(b)   UPI/Corbis-Bettmann

Insert, page 1:
(tl)   Reuters/Corbis-Bettmann
(tr)   Reuters/Corbis-Bettmann
(cr)   Reuters/Corbis-Bettmann
(cl)   Reuters/UPI/Corbis-Bettmann
(bl)   Reuters/Corbis-Bettmann
(br)   Reuters/Corbis-Bettmann

Insert, page 2:
Reuters/Corbis-Bettmann

Insert, page 3:
Reuters/Corbis-Bettmann

Insert, page 4:
Reuters/Corbis-Bettmann

Introduction

At the opening ceremonies of the Olympic Games, each country's athletes parade into the stadium. They are proud, excited, and nervous about the days ahead, just as children are on the first day of school. The excitement begins when an athlete carries one spark to the Olympic torch to set it ablaze.

You can light the Olympic torch that will lead children to a greater understanding and appreciation of math. *OlympicMath* is full of activities to which students can relate. Some activities will help students clarify knowledge they already have. Some activities challenge them to find out more about the world around them. All the activities will require them to think. Students will use their problem-solving, reasoning, and critical-thinking skills as they never have before.

This is no simple drill book. This is math in its most natural form; this is math as it exists in the real world rather than the math many students find isolated on a textbook page. Note that the problems in this book are intended for students in grades 4 through 8 and the problems on

each page are of varying levels of difficulty. The projects in the last half of the book can be done alone or in groups. Our intent is to challenge students to learn more about problem solving—and about the Olympic Games—as they do the math in this book.

References

Lewis, Brad Alan, and Gabriella Goldstein. *Olympic Results—Barcelona 1992*. New York: Garland Publishing, 1993.

Moran, Mike, et al. *The 1984 U. S. Olympic Team Media Guide*. Los Angeles: L.A. Olympic Committee, 1984.

Toomey, Bill, and Barry King. *The Olympic Challenge 1984*. Reston, VA: Reston Publishing Company, 1984.

Wallechinsky, David. *The Complete Book of the Olympics*. Boston: Little, Brown and Company, 1991.

● ● ● ● ●   ● ● ● ● ●   ● ● ● ● ●   ● ● ● ● ●

Contents

From *OlympicMath: Gold Medal Activities and Projects for Grades 4–8* published by GoodYearBooks. Copyright © 1996 Sharon Vogt.

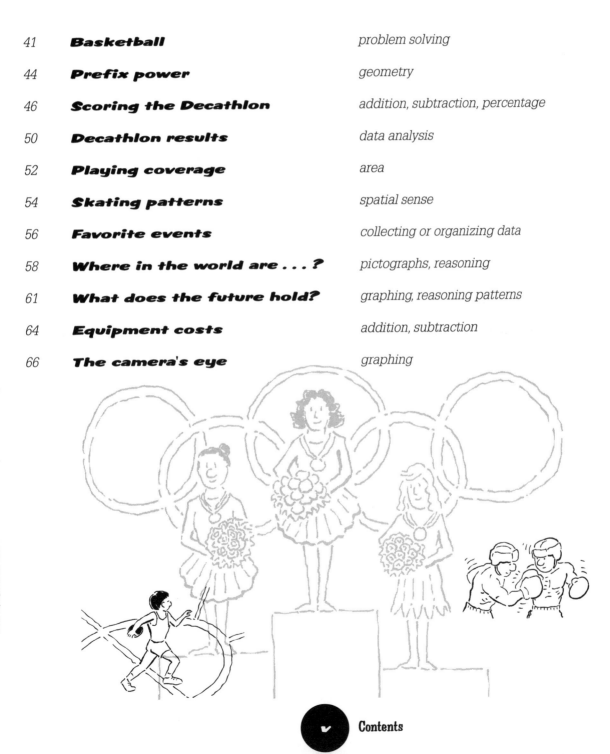

From *OlympicMath: Gold Medal Activities and Projects for Grades 4–8* published by GoodYearBooks. Copyright © 1996 Sharon Vogt.

Contents

● ● ●●●● ● ●●●● ● ●●●● ● ●●●●

ACTIVITIES

Olympic riddles

While covering the Summer Olympic Games for the *Gadzook's Gazette,* Gabe Green took the following notes. As you can see, Gabe is very fond of riddles. You are transcribing Gabe's notes. He has listed the winners' names, each with a corresponding number. To figure out who won each event, use the clues to identify each competitor's number. Write the winners' names in the spaces provided.

Number	Name
56	Ingrid Schafer
27	Eva Bevin
8	Suzanna Haven
117	Carlton Peige
60	Peitro Mendez
11	Joseph Spekinski
65	Brigit Mageste
319	Ralph Jefferson
25	Rob Robertson
88	Rita Hoff

1. Swimming: 50-Meter Freestyle
Three-digit prime number

_____

2. Diving: Platform Diving
Not male
Sum of digits is 9

_____

From *OlympicMath: Gold Medal Activities and Projects for Grades 4–8* published by GoodYearBooks. Copyright © 1996 Sharon Vogt.

Table Tennis: Doubles
Two two-digit numbers
Multiples of 8

_____

_____

4. Yachting: Flying Dutchman, mixed
Two multiples of 5

_____

_____

5. Track and Field: Triple Jump
Multiple of 1, 2, 3, 4, 5, and 6

_____

6. Track and Field: 400-Meter Hurdles
One-digit power of two

_____

7. Badminton: Singles
Not female
Multiple of 3

_____

8. Archery, Individual
Two-digit prime number

_____

From *OlympicMath: Gold Medal Activities and Projects for Grades 4–8* published by GoodYearBooks. Copyright © 1996 Sharon Vogt.

Olympic riddles

Olympic sites

These charts show where the Olympic Games have been held.
Use the information to answer the following questions.

Summer Olympics	
Year	Place
1896	Athens, Greece
1900	Paris, France
1904	St. Louis, U.S.A.
1906	Athens, Greece
1908	London, Great Britain
1912	Stockholm, Sweden
1916	Berlin, Germany*
1920	Antwerp, Belgium
1924	Paris, France
1928	Amsterdam, Holland
1932	Los Angeles, U.S.A.
1936	Berlin, Germany
1940	Tokyo, Japan; Helsinki, Finland*

Olympic events were canceled due to war.

Summer Olympics	
Year	Place
1944	London, Great Britain*
1948	London, Great Britain
1952	Helsinki, Finland
1956	Melbourne, Australia
1960	Rome, Italy
1964	Tokyo, Japan
1968	Mexico City, Mexico
1972	Munich, Germany
1976	Montreal, Canada
1980	Moscow, U.S.S.R.
1984	Los Angeles, U.S.A.
1988	Seoul, South Korea
1992	Barcelona, Spain
1996	Atlanta, U.S.A.

Olympic events were canceled due to war.

1. How many times has the United States hosted Olympic Games?

_____

2. Which countries have hosted the highest number of Winter Olympic Games?

_____

3. Which country has hosted the most Olympic Games *(both summer and winter events)*?

_____

4. How many countries have hosted the Olympics only once *(either summer or winter)*?

_____

From OlympicMath: Gold Medal Activities and Projects for Grades 4-8 published by GoodYearBooks. Copyright © 1996 Sharon Vogt.

Winter Olympics

Year	Place
1924	Chamonix, France
1928	St. Moritz, Switzerland
1932	Lake Placid, U.S.A.
1936	Garmisch-Partenkirchen, Germany
1940	Sapporo, Japan; St. Moritz, Switzerland; Garmisch-Partenkirchen, Germany*
1944	Cortina D'Ampezzo, Italy*
1948	St. Moritz, Switzerland
1952	Oslo, Norway
1956	Cortina D'Ampezzo, Italy
1960	Squaw Valley, U.S.A.
1964	Innsbruck, Austria
1968	Grenoble, France
1972	Sapporo, Japan
1976	Innsbruck, Austria
1980	Lake Placid, U.S.A.
1984	Sarajevo, Yugoslavia
1988	Calgary, Canada
1992	Albertville, France
1994	Lillehammer, Norway
1998	Nagano, Japan

Olympic events were canceled due to war.

5. Could any city in any country host the Olympics? Would there be anything wrong with Houston, Texas, hosting the Winter Olympics?

_____

_____

6. Name two countries where it would not be appropriate to hold the Summer Olympics.

_____

7. Consider the larger countries of the world that have never hosted Olympic Games. Name one country you think should host either the Summer or Winter Olympic Games in the near future. Explain your answer.

_____

_____

From OlympicMath: Gold Medal Activities and Projects for Grades 4–8 published by GoodYearBooks. Copyright © 1996 Sharon Vogt.

Spectators

The chart below shows the seating capacities of the buildings where some of the 1984 Summer Olympic events were held. The third column lists the dates of each event. Use this information to answer the following questions.

1984 Summer Olympics - Los Angeles, CA, U.S.A.

Event	Seating capacity	Dates event held
Archery	4,000	Aug. 8-11
Athletics (Track and Field)	92,604	Aug. 3-6, 8-12
Basketball	17,505	Aug. 7, 10
Boxing	16,000	Aug. 11
Canoeing	10,000	Aug. 10, 11
Cycling	8,000	July 29, 30, Aug. 1, 3, 5
Equestrian	40,000	July 29, 30, Aug. 1, 3, 7-10, 12
Fencing	3,000	Aug. 2-5, 7-9, 11
Field Hockey	22,000	July 31 - Aug. 11
Football (Soccer)	105,000	Aug. 11
Gymnastics	12,500	July 29, 31, Aug. 1-5, 11
Handball	17,505	Aug. 1, 3, 5, 7, 9, 11
Judo	4,200	Aug. 4-11
Rowing	10,000	Aug. 4, 5
Volleyball	11,329	Aug. 7, 11
Weightlifting	4,500	July 29-31, Aug. 1-8
Wrestling	8,892	Aug. 1-3, 9-11

From *OlympicMath: Gold Medal Activities and Projects for Grades 4–8* published by GoodYearBooks. Copyright © 1996 Sharon Vogt.

1. Some of the numbers given for the seating capacities are estimates. Others are exact numbers. For which events are the seating capacities shown probably exact?

_____

_____

2. To which place do most of the remaining numbers seem to be rounded?

_____

3. Round the exact figures to the place named in question 2. Write the rounded figures below.

_____

Use the rounded figures to answer the remaining questions.

4. Which event had the largest seating capacity?

_____

5. In what place is the left-most digit in the value representing the seating capacity for Football?

_____

6. Fencing events were held on several days. If spectators had to purchase one ticket for each day, what is the maximum number of tickets that could be sold?

_____

7. How is the value of the 4 in the seating capacity for Archery events different from the value of the 4 in the seating capacity of Equestrian events?

_____

8. Which event was held on the most number of days?

_____

9. How many tickets could be sold for the event named in question 8?

_____

10. Is the event named in question 8 the one for which the most number of tickets could be sold? If not, which event did have the most number of tickets, and how many tickets were there?

_____

_____

11. Locate the first nonzero digit from the right in the number that describes the seating capacity for Football. In what place is this digit?

_____

From _OlympicMath: Gold Medal Activities and Projects for Grades 4–8_ published by GoodYearBooks. Copyright © 1996 Sharon Vogt.

Medal-winning countries

The chart below records the number of medals won by countries represented at the 1980 and 1984 Summer Olympics. See page 97 for a key to the abbreviations for each country. Note that some countries did not participate in the Olympic Games in 1980, and some did not participate in 1984. Those countries' entries show dashes instead of a number of medals.

Summer, 1980 XXII - Moscow, U.S.S.R.

	G	S	B		G	S	B		G	S	B
ALG	-	-	-	GRE	1	0	2	PER	-	-	-
AUS	2	2	5	GUY	0	0	1	POL	3	14	15
AUT	1	2	1	HOL	0	1	2	POR	-	-	-
BEL	1	0	0	HUN	7	10	15	PRK	0	3	2
BRA	2	0	2	ICE	-	-	-	PUR	-	-	-
BUL	8	16	17	IND	1	0	0	ROM	6	6	13
CAM	-	-	-	IRL	0	1	1	SOV	80	69	46
CAN	-	-	-	ITA	8	3	4	SPA	1	3	2
CHN	-	-	-	IVC	-	-	-	SWE	3	3	6
COL	-	-	-	JAM	0	0	3	SWI	2	0	0
CUB	8	7	5	JPN	-	-	-	SYR	-	-	-
CZE	2	3	9	KEN	-	-	-	TAI	-	-	-
DEN	2	1	2	KOR	-	-	-	TAN	0	2	0
DOM	-	-	-	LEB	0	0	1	THA	-	-	-
EGY	-	-	-	MEX	0	1	3	TUR	-	-	-
ETH	2	0	2	MON	0	2	2	UGA	0	1	0
FIN	3	3	3	MOR	-	-	-	USA	-	-	-
FRA	6	5	13	NGR	-	-	-	VEN	0	1	0
GBR	5	7	9	NOR	-	-	-	YUG	2	3	4
GDR	47	37	42	NZE	-	-	-	ZAM	-	-	-
GER	-	-	-	PAK	-	-	-	ZIM	1	0	0

Summer, 1984 XXIII - Los Angeles, U.S.A.

	G	S	B		G	S	B		G	S	B
ALG	0	0	2	GRE	0	1	1	PER	0	1	0
AUS	4	8	12	GUY	-	-	-	POL	-	-	-
AUT	1	1	1	HOL	5	2	6	POR	1	0	2
BEL	1	1	2	HUN	-	-	-	PRK	-	-	-
BRA	1	5	2	ICE	0	0	1	PUR	0	1	1
BUL	-	-	-	IND	-	-	-	ROM	20	16	17
CAM	0	0	1	IRL	0	1	0	SOV	-	-	-
CAN	10	18	16	ITA	14	6	12	SPA	1	2	2
CHN	15	8	9	IVC	0	1	0	SWE	2	11	6
COL	0	1	0	JAM	0	1	2	SWI	0	4	4
CUB	-	-	-	JPN	10	8	14	SYR	0	1	0
CZE	-	-	-	KEN	1	0	2	TAI	0	0	1
DEN	0	3	3	KOR	6	6	7	TAN	-	-	-
DOM	0	0	1	LEB	-	-	-	THA	0	1	0
EGY	0	1	0	MEX	2	3	1	TUR	0	0	3
ETH	-	-	-	MON	-	-	-	UGA	-	-	-
FIN	4	2	6	MOR	2	0	0	USA	83	61	30
FRA	5	7	16	NGR	0	1	1	VEN	0	0	3
GBR	5	10	22	NOR	0	1	2	YUG	7	4	7
GDR	-	-	-	NZE	8	1	2	ZAM	0	0	1
GER	17	19	23	PAK	1	0	0	ZIM	-	-	-

1. Which country received the most gold medals during the 1984 Summer Olympics?

_____

2. Which country received the most bronze medals during the 1980 Summer Olympics?

_____

Medal-winning countries **10**

From *OlympicMath: Gold Medal Activities and Projects for Grades 4–8* published by GoodYearBooks. Copyright © 1996 Sharon Vogt.

3. Which country received the most medals *(gold, silver, and bronze)* during the 1984 Summer Olympics?

_____

4. Which country received the most medals *(gold, silver, and bronze)* in 1980 and 1984 combined?

_____

5. How many countries received only one gold medal during the 1980 Summer Olympics?

_____

6. How many countries received medals in the 1980 Summer Olympic Games? How many in the 1984 Summer Olympic Games?

_____

_____

7. In which Olympic Games *(1980 or 1984)* did more countries receive medals?

_____

8. What would cause a change in the number of countries who receive medals in the Olympics?

_____

9. During which Olympic Games were more gold medals awarded?

_____

10. What might cause a change in the number of gold medals awarded?

_____

11. Skim through the data in the chart. Did more countries earn more than twenty medals or did more earn twenty or fewer medals *(gold, silver, and bronze)* during the 1984 Summer Olympics?

_____

12. In reference to question 11, do you think this happens in most Olympics? Explain your reasoning.

_____

_____

From *OlympicMath: Gold Medal Activities and Projects for Grades 4–8* published by GoodYearBooks. Copyright © 1996 Sharon Vogt.

Medal-winning greats

Each of the questions below refers to great Olympians who earned many medals during their Olympic careers. Use the information given to answer the questions.

2. In 1968, Mark Spitz won a bronze medal in the 100-Meter Freestyle. His time was 53.0. By how much did he improve his time in 1972?

3. Carl Lewis of the United States was the first man to win two gold medals in the 100-Meter Dash. He won two medals in 1984 and 1988. Wyomia Tyus, also from the U.S., was the first woman to win two gold medals in the 100-Meter Dash. Wyomia earned her medals in 1964 and 1968. How many years before Carl first won the 100-Meter Dash did Wyomia earn her first gold medal?

1. American Mark Spitz was the first Olympic athlete in any sport to win seven gold medals in one Olympics. Competing against Jerry Heidenreich in the 100-Meter Freestyle in 1972, Spitz broke a swimming world record. He completed the 100 meters in 51.22 seconds. Jerry finished second at 51.65 seconds. By what part of a second did Mark win the race?

4. Iolanda Balas of Romania was queen of the high jump from 1957 to 1967. During that time she broke fourteen world records and earned two gold medals. In the Olympic Games in 1960, Iolanda jumped 6-1/16 feet. In 1964, she jumped 6-11/48 feet. In which year did she jump the highest? How much higher (in inches) did she jump?

From *OlympicMath: Gold Medal Activities and Projects for Grades 4–8* published by GoodYearBooks. Copyright © 1996 Sharon Vogt.

6. Wyomia won her first medal by completing the race in 11.4 seconds. she earned her second gold with a time of 11.08 seconds. Carl's times were 9.99 seconds and 9.92 seconds. Imagine the human body having the ability to continue improving at the same rate indefinitely. If Wyomia competed against Carl Lewis in 1984, who would win? Who would win in 1988?

_____

_____

7. Mildred "Babe" Didriksen was declared the greatest female athlete of the first half of the twentieth century. Besides her Olympic honors, Babe was an All-American basketball player, the only female member of an all-male baseball team, and the winner of fourteen straight golf tournaments. In the 1932 Olympics she earned a gold medal for every event she entered. She broke the world record for the 100-Meter Hurdles with a time of 11.7 seconds. In this race, how fast was Babe running in meters per hour? Kilometers per hour?

_____

5. Nadia Comaneci was the star gymnast of the 1976 Olympics. Of the five gymnastic events, Nadia earned medals in four. The women's All-Around competition consists of the horse vault, the uneven bars, the balance beam, and floor exercises. Her scores for these events were 19.625, 20, 19.95, and 19.7. What was Nadia's total score for the All-Around competition?

_____

From *OlympicMath: Gold Medal Activities and Projects for Grades 4–8* published by GoodYearBooks. Copyright © 1996 Sharon Vogt.

Training goals

Sherylin wants to make the track and field team at school. She knows that she will have to run a mile in 8 minutes or less. She also wants to be able to run 100 meters in 20 seconds. Help Sherylin create some realistic goals.

1. Tryouts for the track and field team will be held on April 2. Sherylin will start her own training on January 2. If she trains a little every day, how many days will she have to prepare for the tryouts? *(Assume this is not a leap year.)*

_____

2. Sherylin wants to break her goal into smaller pieces that are easier to achieve. Right now she can run a mile in just under ten minutes. Halfway through her training period, what is the longest amount of time Sherylin should take to run a mile?

_____

3. Sherylin can run 100 meters in 29 seconds. In keeping with her goal, how fast should Sherylin be able to run the distance of 100 meters by March 2?

_____

4. By what day should Sherylin have met 1/5 of her goal?

_____

Following are blank calendar pages. Create a training schedule for Sherylin. Write Sherylin's final goal on the day of the tryouts. Write in her goal time for one mile at every 1/5 and every 1/4 of the way through her training. *(For example, write her goal time at 1/5, 2/5, 3/5, 4/5, and 1/4, 2/4, and 3/4 of the way through her training period.)* Write in her goal time for 100 meters every 1/9 and every 1/3 of the way through her training.

You will use the following calendar pages again for the activities in the next section. Try to write as small and as neatly as possible so that you can add more each day.

January

Training goals

16

February

17   **Training goals**

March

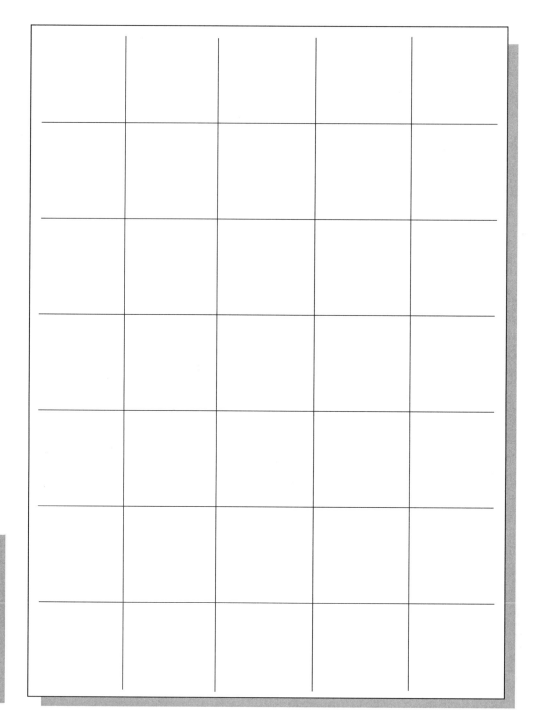

Training goals 18

Training goals

Scheduling

When athletes create training schedules, they usually plan specific activities for alternate days of the week. For example, athletes may work with weights every other day to strengthen their muscles. The remaining days they may spend working on specific skills necessary for their sport.

1. Paula will start her new gymnastics training schedule on March 1. She has planned to lift weights every third day. What is the date of the first day Paula will lift weights? The fifth day? The tenth day?

_____

2. Kevin is training for a swimming meet. He wants to swim laps every other day and run on the treadmill every fifth day. If he starts his training on March 1, how many times will he do both activities on the same day before April 30?

_____

3. In addition to lifting weights, Paula wants to schedule an aerobics session every fourth day. On what date will she lift weights and do aerobics for the first time?

_____

4. Paula works out in the gym every day except Sunday. Depending on her weightlifting and aerobics schedule, she could have the day off. If March 7 is a Sunday, how many Sundays will Paula have a break from training between March 1 and April 30?

_____

Challenge problems

5. Kevin and Paula want to work together on the weights about once a week. Kevin wants to plan more days on the weights than does Paula. How can Kevin plan his schedule to make this possible?

_____

_____

6. Sherylin is planning specific activities to include in her training schedule. In the previous section you created a calendar for Sherylin to remind her of her goals. Use that same calendar to note the activities she will do each day. Sherylin plans to run one mile every day. She wants the following activities included in her training schedule as reminders. Draw a symbol for each activity on appropriate days: Lift weights every fifth day; run the stairs at school every fourth day, starting with six flights and adding an additional flight every two times; time herself running 100 meters every third day.

From *OlympicMath: Gold Medal Activities and Projects for Grades 4–8* published by GoodYearBooks. Copyright © 1996 Sharon Vogt.

Gymnastics

International gymnastic competitions include three different levels. Each level involves either individual or team competition. A team consists of six gymnasts from one nation. During the first level of competition, every individual performs each event. Scores for team members are combined. Teams with the highest scores are declared winners of the team competition. Individual scores from the first level of competition are ranked from highest to lowest. The top thirty-six scorers go on to compete in the second level of competition. During this second level, also known as the All-Around, the gymnasts again perform each event. The three gymnasts with the highest scores receive medals for the All-Around competition. Finally, the gymnasts' scores for the first two levels of competition are combined. The eight gymnasts with the highest combined scores compete in the third level of competition. The athletes perform each event a third time, but this time the scores received in each event are compared. Medals are awarded to the top three scorers in each separate event.

The charts on the next page show individual scores for the Gymnast Internationals' first level of competition. The Gymnast Internationals is a competition that helps gymnasts prepare for the Olympics. Complete the charts by filling in the total score for each competitor. Use this data to answer the questions that follow.

From OlympicMath: Gold Medal Activities and Projects for Grades 4–8 published by GoodYearBooks. Copyright © 1996 Sharon Vogt.

Gymnast Internationals - Men's competition

Name	Nation	HB	PB	LHV	SH	R	FE	Total
Louis Bonvi	FRA	19.8	19.8	19.7	19.85	19.875	19.6	
Koji Kaji	JPN	19.9	19.8	19.85	19.725	19.75	19.6	
Tong Ning	CHN	19.975	19.625	19.725	19.9	19.8	19.825	
Ken Gaylord	USA	19.625	19.85	19.825	19.775	19.875	19.575	
Xu Fei	CHN	19.8	19.775	19.725	19.875	19.775	19.3	
Yukio Kato	JPN	19.3	19.4	19.475	19.825	19.8	19.95	
Vlad Titov	SOV	19.725	19.6	19.8	19.7	19.725	19.675	
George Niles	USA	19.8	19.8	19.425	19.475	19.675	19.775	
Grant Murov	SOV	19.4	18.85	18.75	19.0	18.85	18.95	
Masao Ono	JPN	19.6	19.1	18.5	19.2	19.05	18.75	

HB = Horizontal Bars, PB = Parallel Bars, LHV = Long Horse Vault, SH = Side Horse,
R = Rings, FE = Floor Exercises

1. List the top six male gymnasts for the Long Horse Vault in order from highest score to lowest score.

_____

_____

_____

_____

_____

_____

2. List the top six female gymnasts on the Balance Beam in order from highest score to lowest score.

_____

_____

_____

_____

_____

_____

Gymnastics **22**

From OlympicMath: Gold Medal Activities and Projects for Grades 4–8 published by GoodYearBooks. Copyright © 1996 Sharon Vogt.

Gymnast Internationals - Women's competition

Name	Nation	HV	AB	BB	FE	Total
Yelena Kim	SOV	19.625	19.925	19.65	19.875	
Emilia Pauca	ROM	19.85	19.5	19.85	19.925	
Ma Yongyan	CHN	19.725	19.3	19.95	19.55	
Bonnie Nea	USA	19.8	19.887	19.325	19.762	
Chen Ping	CHN	19.525	19.275	19.5	19.425	
Nadia Szabó	ROM	19.675	19.725	19.8	19.875	
Julie McNim	USA	19.887	19.862	19.837	19.95	
Steffi Kerst	HUN	19.8	19.887	19.85	19.762	
Olga Janz	HUN	18.7	19.3	18.85	19.15	
Nelli Burda	SOV	19.85	19.725	19.3	19.8	

HV = Horse Vault, AB = Asymmetrical (uneven) bars,
BB = Balance Beam, FE = Floor Exercises

3. In this competition, the team score is determined by combining the highest scores in each event. List the gold, silver, and bronze-medal winning countries for the Men's and Women's Team Competition along with each team's winning score.

Men's team competition

Place	Nation	Score
Gold	_____	_____
Silver	_____	_____
Bronze	_____	_____

Women's team competition

Place	Nation	Score
Gold	_____	_____
Silver	_____	_____
Bronze	_____	_____

Nordic skiing great

Over an eight-year period that encompassed three Winter Olympics, Sixten Jernberg earned nine medals in Nordic Skiing. Of these medals, four were gold, three silver, and two bronze. Nordic, or cross-country, skiers race against the clock. They use two techniques in these events: the classical, consisting of a diagonal stride, and freestyle, which has no restrictions. Freestyle skiers use a faster "skating" style.

Use the clues given here to discover the event and the year in which Sixten earned each medal. In each box of the chart, write the type of medal won *(gold, silver, or bronze)* or "none" to indicate that Sixten didn't win a medal at all. You will need to refer to the chart on page 4 for help with some clues.

Clues:
1. In 1956, Sixten won the only bronze medal his country received.
2. The only Games in which Sixten won medals in every event he entered were held in Italy.
3. Gold is the only medal that Sixten won in every Olympics.
4. In the Olympics held in the United States, Sixten only won two medals.
5. Sixten won two gold medals in the race that covers 50,000 meters.
6. In Austria, Sixten won two gold medals and a bronze.
7. Sixten won his second bronze in the 15 Kilometers *(classical).*
8. Practice pays. Sixten won a bronze medal in the relay one year only to come back eight years later and win the gold.
9. The 15 Kilometers was the only event in which Sixten didn't win a gold.
10. Sixten won his gold medal for the 30 Kilometers in the United States. This is the only gold medal he won that year.
11. The 15,000,000–millimeter race was the only event in which Sixten won a medal each year.

Event	1956	1960	1964
15 Kilometers (classical)			
30 Kilometers (classical)			
50 Kilometers (freestyle)			
4 x 10-Kilometer Relay			

From *OlympicMath: Gold Medal Activities and Projects for Grades 4–8* published by GoodYearBooks. Copyright © 1996 Sharon Vogt.

Running events

Track and Field includes more events than any other sport competitions in the Olympics. The events involving running are:

100 Meters
200 Meters
400 Meters
800 Meters
1,500 Meters
3,000 Meters
5,000 Meters
10,000 Meters
Marathon *(42,195 meters)*
100-Meter Hurdles
110-Meter Hurdles
400-Meter Hurdles
3000-Meter Steeplechase
4 x 100-Meter Relay
4 x 400-Meter Relay
Pentathlon *(200 Meters and 80-Meter Hurdles)*
Decathlon *(100 Meters, 400 Meters, 1,500 Meters, and 110-
   Meter Hurdles)*

1/1,000 kilometer *(km)* = 1/100 hectometer *(hm)* =
1/10 decameter *(dam)* = 1 meter (m) = 10 decimeter *(dm)* =
100 centimeter *(cm)* =1,000 millimeter *(mm)*

Notice that all Olympic races are measured using the metric system. This was the system of measurement in use in Europe when the Olympics first began. Use what you know about the metric system to answer the following questions.

1. Which race covers a distance of 100,000 mm?

_____

2. Which race covers a distance of 150 dam?

_____

3. How many kilometers must an athlete run in the 10,000 Meters?

_____

4. How many centimeters must an athlete run in the 110-Meter Hurdles competition?

_____

5. In the 4 x 400-Meter Relay, four team members each run 400 meters. How many kilometers does the team run altogether?

_____

6. If the 200 Meters was broken up into a relay race for four team members, how many decimeters would each person run?

_____

7. How many decameters does an athlete run in the Decathlon?

_____

8. How many hectometers does an athlete run in the Pentathlon?

_____

For a better idea of the differences between the distances of each race, you can draw a diagram of a race to scale.

9. Draw one line for each of the following races measuring one centimeter for every 100 meters an athlete would run.

100 Meters
200 Meters
400 Meters
800 Meters
1,500 Meters
110-Meter Hurdles
4 x 100-Meter Relay
4 x 400-Meter Relay
Pentathlon

10. Draw one line for each of the following races measuring one millimeter for every 100 meters an athlete would run.

3,000 Meters
5,000 Meters
10,000 Meters
Decathlon

How long?

In the previous section you compared the distances of a few of the Track and Field running events. You got an idea of how the lengths of these courses compare. But exactly how far does an athlete run in a marathon? Use what you know about the metric system to estimate. Circle the more appropriate estimate for each distance.

1. 100 meters?

2. 1,500 meters?

3. 10,000 meters?

4. The marathon run in the Olympics is 42,195 meters. One kilometer equals about 0.62 miles. Approximately how many miles does an athlete run in a marathon?

_____

Challenge problem

5. Find a map of your town and use it to plan a route to be used for an Olympic marathon. The scale of the map will describe the lengths of streets in your area. Using the scale, map out a route that is about 42,195 meters. If the map shows distances in miles, use the distance you calculated in problem 4. Once you have decided on your route, make a map of the route on a piece of paper. Remember that marathons usually do not begin and end at the same location so you do not have to plan a circular route.

From *OlympicMath: Gold Medal Activities and Projects for Grades 4–8* published by GoodYearBooks. Copyright © 1996 Sharon Vogt.

Using a stopwatch

In Olympic events, competitors are so evenly matched in skill that often the athlete who claims the gold may win by only a small margin. In timed events, the gold-medal winner may cross the finish line only a fraction of a second before the silver medalist. Therefore, accurate timing devices are very important. When athletes are training, they must also have accurate timing devices to know exactly how they compare against the competition.

Stopwatches display time in minutes and seconds. *(In years past, time couldn't be recorded to the nearest tenth, but now Olympic times are shown with greater accuracy using more precise devices.)* The readout of a stopwatch may look like the stopwatch shown in the drawing. The two zeros farthest to the left are the place holders for minutes. The two middle zeros are the place holders for seconds. The two zeros farthest to the right represent fractions of a second. If the stopwatch read 02:37.58, that would mean a time of 2 minutes and 37.58 seconds, or 2 minutes, 37 and 58/100 seconds.

Use what you know about place value and time to answer the following questions.

1. In 1920, Albert Hill ran the 800 Meters in the time shown on the stopwatch. The silver medalist, Earl Eby, completed the race two-tenths of a second behind Albert. How long did it take Earl to complete the race?

_____

2. In 1972, Yulia Ryabchinskaya completed the 500-Meter Kayak event in the time shown. Mieke Jaapies finished the race 86/100 of a second later. What was Mieke's time?

_____

From *OlympicMath: Gold Medal Activities and Projects for Grades 4–8* published by GoodYearBooks. Copyright © 1996 Sharon Vogt.

3. Fredy Schmidtke completed the 1984 1,000-Meter Cycling time trial in 1:06.10. The silver medalist from Canada completed the race in 1:06.44. By what portion of a second did Fredy win the race?

_____

4. The Italian Sculls rowing team completed the course in 5:53.37 in 1988. The Norwegian team followed closely with a time of 5:55.08. How much more time did the Norwegian team take to complete the event?

_____

5. Alfréd Hajós set an Olympic swimming record in 1896 by completing the 100-Meter Freestyle in 1:22.2. In 1988, Matthew Biodi set another Olympic record for the event with a time of 48.63. By how much was the Olympic record improved between 1896 and 1988?

_____

6. Women were allowed to compete in swimming events for the first time in 1912. The first female 100-Meter Freestyle gold medalist completed the event in the same amount of time as Alfréd Hajós had in 1896. The gold medalist in 1980 set a world record with a time of 54.79. By how much time did the women's Olympic record improve between 1912 and 1980?

_____

Some events require more than 60 minutes to complete. For these events, a different timer must be used with a readout that includes hours. Times for these events are shown in this format: 00:00:00.00.

7. In the 1972 Marathon, Frank Shorter ran 14,750 meters in a time of 2:12:19.8. The world's best time for the event was 2:08:33.6. By how much time did Frank miss setting a new record?

Challenge problem

8. The 4 x 10-Kilometer Nordic Relay is a team race. Each team member skis 10 kilometers. In 1975, the gold medalists completed the race with a time of 2:07:59.72. The second-place team had a time of 2:09:58.36. By how much time did the first-place team win?

From *OlympicMath: Gold Medal Activities and Projects for Grades 4–8* published by GoodYearBooks. Copyright © 1996 Sharon Vogt.

Tracking track events

Many Track and Field events include several rounds of competition before the final race. These rounds serve to eliminate competitors. The rounds and their qualifications vary depending on the number of competitors. In the 1992 Olympics, the Women's 200 Meters consisted of four rounds. In the first round, seven or eight competitors at a time ran track heats until all had run. The first four in each heat to cross the finish line qualified to continue. In addition, the best four times *(other than those who already qualified)* in all heats combined also qualified. In the second round, the qualified athletes competed against each other again with the first four in each race qualifying to continue competition. Next the qualified athletes competed in the semifinals. Again, the first four to finish qualified for the finals. The winners of the final race earned medals.

The chart below shows the running times of the final competitors in the 1992 Summer Olympics. Use the chart and the information above to answer the questions that follow.

Name	Nation	Round 1	Round 2	Semifinal	Final
Gwen Torrence	USA	22.66	22.21	21.72	21.81
Juliet Cuthbert	JAM	22.99	22.01	21.75	22.02
Merlene Ottey	JAM	22.95	21.94	22.12	22.09
Irina Privalova	EUN	23.22	22.45	22.08	22.19
Carlette Guidry	USA	22.82	22.26	22.31	22.3
Grace Jackson Small	JAM	22.72	22.59	22.58	22.58
Michelle Finn	USA	23.00	22.42	22.39	22.61
Galina Malchugina	EUN	23.08	22.22	22.44	22.63

All times are shown in seconds.

From OlympicMath: Gold Medal Activities and Projects for Grades 4–8 published by GoodYearBooks. Copyright © 1996 Sharon Vogt.

1. If the final eight runners had competed against each other in the first round, which four would have qualified?

_____

2. Which competitor had the best average time? What was the average?

_____

3. Merlene Ottey came in first in every race but the final. How much did her total time in all four races differ from Gwen's total time?

_____

4. Juliet Cuthbert took the silver medal in the 100 Meters as well. Her time in the final was 10.83 seconds. How much greater was her average time per 100 meters in the 200 Meters?

_____

The chart below shows the amount of time it took the top ten competitors in the Women's Marathon at the 1992 Olympics to reach the 5-kilometer and 20-kilometer marks. The total distance of the Marathon was 42,195 meters. Use the data to solve the problems that follow.

Name	Nation	5 km	20 km	Final
V. Yegorova	EUN	18:23	1:14:14	2:32:41
Yuko Arimori	JPN	18:00	—	2:32:49
L. Moller	NZL	18:16	1:14:16	2:33:59
S. Yamachita	JPN	18:01	1:14:13	2:36:26
Katrin Doerre	GER	17:59	1:14:13	2:36:48
Gyong-ae Mun	PRK	18:16	1:14:14	2:37:03
M. Machado	POR	17:59	1:14:10	2:38:22
R. Burangulova	EUN	18:04	1:14:19	2:38:46
C. De Reuck	RSA	18:00	1:14:12	2:39:03
Cathy O'Brien	USA	18:18	1:15:25	2:39:42

5. If the competitors could have kept up the speed they had attained at the 5-kilometer mark, who would have come in first?

_____

6. What was the difference between the time it took the first- and third-place competitors to cross the finish line?

_____

7. The last competitor crossed the finish line with a time of 3:29:10. How much longer did it take this athlete to finish the race than the first-place winner?

_____

From OlympicMath: Gold Medal Activities and Projects for Grades 4–8 published by GoodYearBooks. Copyright © 1996 Sharon Vogt.

Challenge problems

8. What was the gold medalist's average speed in kilometers per hour for the first 20 kilometers and for the entire race?

_____

9. If Cathy O'Brien had finished the last portion of the race with the same average time as her first 20 kilometers, at about what time would she have crossed the finish line?

_____

Who won?

Use logic and reasoning skills to determine the gold, silver, and bronze medalists for each of the events described below.

1. An eighth-grade class organized a badminton competition. Sixteen teams *(numbered 1 through 16)* competed. Team 1 and teams with numbers that are multiples of 3 or 5 were eliminated in the first round. In the second round, team 2 and all the remaining odd-numbered teams were eliminated. In the semifinals, the highest numbered team remaining played the lowest and the team with the two-digit number won. The other two teams competed and the team with the number that's a multiple of seven won. In the final play-off, the team with a number that is a power of two won. In badminton, the gold medal is awarded to the winner of the final play-off. The silver is awarded to the gold medalist's final competitor, and bronze medals are awarded to the remaining two teams in the semifinals.

Gold Medalist: _____

Silver Medalist: _____

Bronze Medalist: _____

From *OlympicMath: Gold Medal Activities and Projects for Grades 4–8* published by GoodYearBooks. Copyright © 1996 Sharon Vogt.

2. The middle-school swim team organized its own competition. In a 200-meter butterfly race, eight students competed. Tom didn't finish first. Kym received a medal. Bob and Jaime tied for last. Wendy was just short of receiving the bronze. Paul and Ona came in right behind Wendy. Madeline came in behind Kym but ahead of Tom.

Gold Medalist: _____

Silver Medalist: _____

Bronze Medalist: _____

3. Six students competed in the 100-meter freestyle. Nigel and Sara tied. Peter finished right before them, and two students finished before Peter. No one had a greater time than Ken. Sue finished after John.

Gold Medalist: _____

Silver Medalist: _____

Bronze Medalist: _____

4. Four teams competed in a 4 x 100-meter freestyle relay. Team 1 didn't finish first or last. Team 2 finished right before team 3. Team 4 didn't finish last.

Gold Medalist: _____

Silver Medalist: _____

Bronze Medalist: _____

Challenge problem

5. The Archery Club organized a competition. Eight students competed. A competitor could earn a maximum total of 120 points. Todd missed the maximum number of points by 22. Cindy earned the smallest number of points possible that is a multiple of 2, 5, and 7. Ben scored the largest number of points possible that is a factor of 600 and 780. Nick scored less points than Ben. José's points totaled the same as the average of Todd's, Cindy's, and Ben's points. Cheryl earned 1 less point than Ben. Maxine earned less points than Todd but more than José. Pauleen's total points added up to the largest power of 2 possible.

Gold Medalist: _____

Silver Medalist: _____

Bronze Medalist: _____

From *OlympicMath: Gold Medal Activities and Projects for Grades 4–8* published by GoodYearBooks. Copyright © 1996 Sharon Vogt.

The volleyball court

A regulation volleyball court measures 60 feet by 30 feet. It is divided in half by a net. The net extends one foot beyond each sideline. In men's play, the net is eight feet high. In women's play, the net is 7 feet 4-1/2 inches. Both nets are 3 feet deep. A line extends from one sideline to the other 10 feet from the centerline on both sides of the net. The back-row players are not allowed to touch or cross this line when they spike.

Draw a diagram of a volleyball court to scale in the space below. One scale that will allow the diagram to fit on this page is to let 1 inch represent 15 feet. Label each line with actual and scale measurements. If possible, after making the diagram, use masking tape or chalk to mark off a regulation court in a gymnasium or on a field.

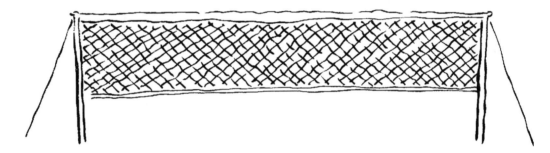

Archery

In Olympic competition, athletes shoot 288 arrows over the course of four days. They shoot from four different distances from the target. The target is made up of ten circles all having the same center. If an arrow lands in the innermost circle, the athlete earns ten points. Each circle beyond the center circle is worth one less point than the previous circle. An arrow that lands in the outermost circle earns the athlete only one point.

1. Patricia shot five arrows to earn a total score of 30. Draw arrows on the target below to show one way her arrows could have landed on the target.

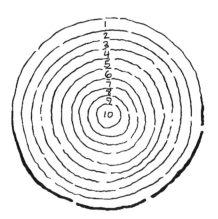

3. Ryan shot seven arrows and earned a score of 56. If all of Ryan's arrows landed in the same section, how many points did he earn for each arrow?

_____

2. Draw another way Patricia's arrows could have landed on the target.

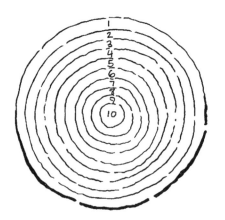

4. If one of Ryan's arrows had landed in the innermost circle and another in the next circle out, by how much would his score increase?

_____

From *OlympicMath: Gold Medal Activities and Projects for Grades 4–8* published by GoodYearBooks. Copyright © 1996 Sharon Vogt.

Speed skating

In several Olympic events, the winner is the first to cross the finish line. In these races, athletes compete against each other, sometimes edging out their competitors in the last minute. But speed skaters race against the clock. Two skaters complete the course at the same time. After all skaters have raced, final times are compared to determine a winner.

1. In the 1932 Winter Olympics, Speed Skating competitions were held as actual races similar to running and swimming competitions. Five or six skaters competed against each other in qualifying heats for the 500 Meters. This method of competition is known as North American Rules because the rules originated in North America. Five of the six athletes who competed in the final heat were North Americans. Athletes from other countries didn't like to compete under these rules and protested. North American Rules have never been used since. Why did this slight change in rules negatively affect many speed skaters' performances?

_____

_____

_____

_____

The chart below gives winning times (in minutes and seconds) for the 1,000-Meter Speed Skating event. It also shows times for other 1,000-meter events. Use the data to answer the questions.

Event	Gold	Silver	Bronze
Speed Skating	1:52.06	1:52.12	1:52.31
Canoeing - Kayak singles	3:45.73	3:46.88	3:47.38
Canoeing - Kayak fours	3:00.20	3:01.40	3:02.37
Canoeing - Canadian singles	4:12.78	4:15.83	4:18.94
Canoeing - Canadian pairs	3:48.36	3:51.44	3:54.33
Cycling - Time trial	1:04.499	1:04.784	1:05.114

2. In which event do the athletes complete the 1,000-meter course in the least amount of time?

_____

3. In which Canoeing event do the athletes complete the 1,000-meter course in the least amount of time?

_____

4. What is the accuracy of the time shown for all events but the Cycling event?

_____

5. What is the greatest possible error in the time shown for the Cycling event?

_____

6. In the Canoeing events, did an individual or teams complete the races in less time?

_____

7. Explain one way in which the number of people in a canoe can change the speed at which the canoe travels.

_____

_____

8. Give one reason why some events need more accurate timing devices than others.

_____

_____

Challenge problem

9. What was the approximate average speed in kilometers per hour of the gold-medal Cycling competitor?

_____

From OlympicMath: Gold Medal Activities and Projects for Grades 4-8 published by GoodYearBooks. Copyright © 1996 Sharon Vogt.

Basketball

The United States has dominated Olympic Basketball competitions since 1936, the very first year men's basketball was added to the Games. In every Summer Olympics from 1936 to 1968, the American men's basketball team came home with the gold. In 1972, it took the silver medal, then it took the gold again in 1976. Women's basketball was first entered in the Olympics in 1976. Except for 1980, the U.S. women's team has also taken a medal in each competition since then.

   In the box on the next page are the scores for the games the United States Men's Olympic Basketball team played during their eight-time Olympic winning streak. Use the data to answer the questions that follow.

1936	1956	USA 86–53 BRA
USA 52–28 EST	USA 98–40 JPN	USA 116–50 KOR
USA 56–23 PHI	USA 101–29 THA	USA 62–42 PUR
USA 25–10 MEX	USA 121–53 PHI	USA 73–59 SOV
USA 19–08 CAN	USA 84–44 BUL	
	USA 85–55 SOV	1968
1948	USA 101–38 URU	USA 81–46 SPA
USA 86–21 SWI	USA 89–55 SOV	USA 93–36 SEN
USA 53–28 CZE		USA 96–75 PHI
USA 59–57 ARG	1960	USA 73–58 YUG
USA 66–28 EGY	USA 88–54 ITA	USA 95–50 PAN
USA 61–33 PER	USA 125–66 JPN	USA 100–61 ITA
USA 63–28 URU	USA 107–63 HUN	USA 61–56 PUR
USA 71–40 MEX	USA 104–42 YUG	USA 75–63 BRA
USA 65–21 FRA	USA 108–50 URU	USA 65–50 YUG
	USA 81–57 SOV	
1952	USA 112–81 ITA	1972
USA 66–48 HUN	USA 90–63 BRA	USA 65–35 CZE
USA 72–47 CZE		USA 81–55 AUS
USA 57–44 URU	1964	USA 67–48 CUB
USA 86–58 SOV	USA 78–45 AUS	USA 61–54 BRA
USA 103–55 CHI	USA 77–51 FIN	USA 96–31 EGY
USA 57–53 BRA	USA 60–45 PER	USA 72–56 SPA
USA 85–86 ARG	USA 83–28 URU	USA 99–33 JPN
USA 36–25 SOV	USA 69–61 YUG	USA 68–38 ITA

From OlympicMath: Gold Medal Activities and Projects for Grades 4–8 published by GoodYearBooks. Copyright © 1996 Sharon Vogt.

1. During its four games, how many points did the U.S. Basketball team score in 1936?

_____

2. Of all the points scored in those four games in 1936, what percent of the points were scored by the United States?

_____

3. The last game listed for each year is the final match. Which country has contended most often against the United States for the gold?

_____

4. The teams entering into the basketball competition are divided into two groups. Each of the teams within a group plays the others in the first round of competition. The four teams with the best winning records play each other in a final round to determine the medal winners. How many teams entered the 1960 Olympic competition?

_____

5. How many basketball games were played during the first round of the 1960 Olympics?

_____

6. What was the United States' average score for games played in the 1972 Olympics?

_____

7. On a separate sheet of paper, draw a graph showing the total points scored by the United States team during each Olympic competition. Choose the most appropriate graph to display the data.

_____

8. Why do you think the scores were lower in 1936 than in any other year? Why might the United States have played its fewest number of games that year?

_____

_____

Challenge problem

9. Using estimation, determine the year in which the United States team scored the most points in all its games combined.

_____

43 Basketball

Prefix power

Understanding prefixes can help you interpret the names of some of the Olympic events. The words for the events start with prefixes you might recognize. You may have seen them when working with shapes.

Decathlon

Biathlon

Heptathlon

Modern Pentathlon

From *OlympicMath: Gold Medal Activities and Projects for Grades 4–8* published by GoodYearBooks. Copyright © 1996 Sharon Vogt.

Write the number represented by each of the following prefixes.

1. deca _____

2. hepta _____

3. penta _____

4. bi _____

5. octa _____

6. quad _____

7. hexa _____

8. nona _____

Use what you know about prefixes to write the name of each shape drawn below.

12.

_____

9.

_____

13.

_____

10.

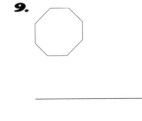

_____

Challenge problem

14.

11.

_____

Scoring the Decathlon

The winners of many Olympic events must cross the finish line first. Others win by throwing or jumping the farthest. In the Decathlon, Heptathlon, and Modern Pentathlon, the winners must earn the most points. For these three events, judges are given extremely detailed scoring tables defining the performance required to earn each point. The table below shows three examples of points earned in each event. Use the information in the table to answer the questions that follow.

Decathlon scoring guide

Event	600 points	800 points	1,000 points
100 Meters	12.0 sec	11.1 sec	10.3 sec
Long Jump	5.98 m	6.90 m	7.90 m
Shot Put	12.01 m	15.19 m	18.75 m
High Jump	1.71 m	1.93 m	2.17 m
400 Meters	55.1 sec	50.2 sec	46.0 sec
110-Meter Hurdles	17.8 sec	15.5 sec	13.7 sec
Discus	35.77 m	45.99 m	57.5 m
Pole Vault	3.24 m	3.97 m	4.78 m
Javelin	47.56 m	63.17 m	81.00 m
1,500 Meters	4 min 28.4 sec	4 min 2.0 sec	3 min 40.2 sec

From OlympicMath: Gold Medal Activities and Projects for Grades 4-8 published by GoodYearBooks. Copyright © 1996 Sharon Vogt.

1. How many points would an athlete receive for completing the 110-Meter Hurdles in 5.5 seconds?

_____

2. What length must an athlete jump in the High Jump competition in order to earn 1,000 points?

_____

3. If an athlete threw a javelin 55.37 m, about how many points do you think he or she would earn?

_____

4. What finishing time do you think it would take to earn 900 points in the 1,500 Meters?

_____

5. Sam's final point total was 9,562. How many points did Sam average in each event?

_____

6. Sam earned 1,200 points in the Long Jump competition. What percent of his total came from these points?

_____

7. All athletes have competed in all events except the 1,500 Meters. José is currently in second place with a score of 8,250. The first-place athlete has a score of 8,450. If José earns 1,000 points in this event, under what time must the first-place competitor complete the 1,500 Meters for José to take the gold?

_____

8. Peter ran the 100 Meters in 11.1 seconds, the 400 Meters in 55.1 seconds, and the 1,500 Meters in 3 minutes 40.2 seconds. His total score after completing all events was 9,750. What percent of his score came from the running events?

_____

Several students at Thadley Middle School decided to organize their own decathlon. Here are the competitors and their results for each event. You are the judge. How many points did each athlete earn? After calculating each athlete's points, determine the place *(1st, 2nd, etc.)* in which each finished.

9. Todd Newman
    100 Meters - 11.1 sec
    Long Jump - 5.98 m
    Shot Put - 12.01 m
    High Jump - 1.93 m
    400 Meters - 50.2 sec
    110-Meter Hurdles - 13.7 sec
    Discus - 45.99 m
    Pole Vault - 4.78 m
    Javelin - 63.17 m
    1,500 Meters - 4 min 2 sec

    Total Score: _____

    Place: _____

11. Bobby Schwartz
    100 Meters - 11.1 sec
    Long Jump - 7.90 m
    Shot Put - 15.19 m
    High Jump - 2.17 m
    400 Meters - 55.1 sec
    110-Meter Hurdles - 17.8 sec
    Discus - 57.5 m
    Pole Vault - 3.97 m
    Javelin - 63.17 m
    1,500 Meters - 4 min 2 sec

    Total Score: _____

    Place: _____

10. Katie Staples
    100 Meters - 10.3 sec
    Long Jump - 5.98 m
    Shot Put - 15.19 m
    High Jump - 1.71 m
    400 Meters - 55.1 sec
    110-Meter Hurdles - 17.8 sec
    Discus - 45.99 m
    Pole Vault - 3.24 m
    Javelin - 81.00 m
    1,500 Meters - 4 min 28.4 sec

    Total Score: _____

    Place: _____

12. Christina Pendleton
    100 Meters - 10.3 sec
    Long Jump - 7.90 m
    Shot Put - 12.01 m
    High Jump - 2.17 m
    400 Meters - 46.0 sec
    110-Meter Hurdles - 13.7 sec
    Discus - 45.99 m
    Pole Vault - 3.24 m
    Javelin - 47.56 m
    1,500 Meters - 3 min 40.2 sec

    Total Score: _____

    Place: _____

From *OlympicMath: Gold Medal Activities and Projects for Grades 4–8* published by GoodYearBooks. Copyright © 1996 Sharon Vogt.

13. Ken Whitehead

    100 Meters - 12.0 sec

    Long Jump - 7.90 m

    Shot Put - 15.19 m

    High Jump - 2.17 m

    400 Meters - 55.1 sec

    110-Meter Hurdles - 17.8 sec

    Discus - 45.99 m

    Pole Vault - 3.97 m

    Javelin - 63.17 m

    1,500 Meters - 4 min 28.4 sec

    Total Score: _____

    Place: _____

14. Kimberly Donovan

    100 Meters - 10.3 sec

    Long Jump - 6.90 m

    Shot Put - 12.01 m

    High Jump - 2.17 m

    400 Meters - 46.0 sec

    110-Meter Hurdles - 15.5 sec

    Discus - 35.77 m

    Pole Vault - 3.24 m

    Javelin - 47.56 m

    1,500 Meters - 4 min 2 sec

    Total Score: _____

    Place: _____

From *OlympicMath: Gold Medal Activities and Projects for Grades 4–8* published by GoodYearBooks. Copyright © 1996 Sharon Vogt.

Decathlon results

Athletes can learn much about their performance by analyzing their results. A few students from Thadley Middle School competed in a decathlon. In the previous section you determined their total points. Use their scores as data in the following activities.

1. To analyze his results, Todd wants to see them in a bar graph. Make a bar graph showing the points Todd earned in each event of the decathlon.

3. Katie Staples wants to see a circle graph showing the points she earned in the ten events in the decathlon. Make a circle graph in the space below.

2. Describe one thing Todd can conclude about his performance based on the bar graph.

_____

_____

4. Describe one thing Katie can learn about her performance based on the circle graph.

_____

_____

From *OlympicMath: Gold Medal Activities and Projects for Grades 4–8* published by GoodYearBooks. Copyright © 1996 Sharon Vogt.

5. Bobby wants to improve his performance so that in the next competition he has a better chance of placing above Christina. What type of graph can he make to help him? What helpful information will this graph show?

_____

_____

_____

_____

_____

_____

_____

_____

Playing coverage

Many sports are played on rectangular playing surfaces of various sizes. The number of athletes on a team varies with each sport. So, the area for which a player is responsible also varies.

Calculate the total area of the unique playing field for each sport listed here. Then determine the area one player has to cover if each player is responsible for the same amount of space. Disregard goalies in sports that require them since they are only responsible for the area near the goal.

1. Football *(Soccer)*
Team: 10 players, 1 goalie

Area: _____

Player coverage: _____

2. Handball *(Team)*

Team: 6 players, 1 goalie

Area: _____

Player coverage: _____

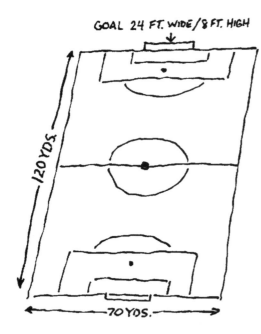

GOAL 24 FT. WIDE/8 FT. HIGH

120 YDS.

70 YDS.

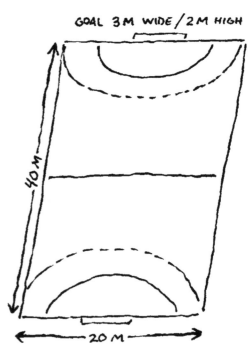

GOAL 3 M WIDE/2 M HIGH

40 M

20 M

From *OlympicMath: Gold Medal Activities and Projects for Grades 4–8* published by GoodYearBooks. Copyright © 1996 Sharon Vogt.

3. Hockey

Team: 10 players, 1 goalie

Area: _____

Player coverage: _____

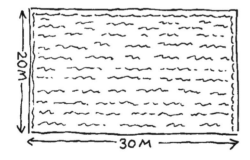

4. Water Polo

Team: 6 players, 1 goalie

Area: _____

Player coverage: _____

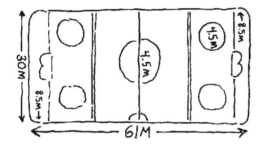

5. Volleyball

Team: 6 players

Area: _____

Player coverage: _____

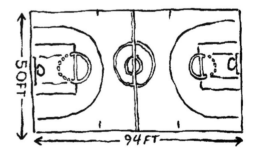

6. Basketball

Team: 5 players

Area: _____

Player coverage: _____

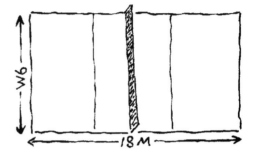

From *OlympicMath: Gold Medal Activities and Projects for Grades 4–8* published by GoodYearBooks. Copyright © 1996 Sharon Vogt.

Skating patterns

In Olympic Games prior to 1992, the first requirement of figure skaters was to skate several mandatory *(called* compulsory *in this sport)* figures. One of these figures was the figure eight. After each performance, judges examined the marks the skater left on the ice, looking for a figure eight that was perfectly round and balanced. The judges examined the other compulsory figures just as carefully, rewarding perfection with the highest scores. Compulsory figures were eliminated from Olympic Figure Skating in 1992.

Imagine what your daily movements would look like if you could examine them as the judges examined the skaters' movements. Draw lines to represent the movements you make in each of the following situations.

1. walking or riding to school

2. going from the math classroom to the gym

3. doing a household chore

4. playing your favorite sport

From *OlympicMath: Gold Medal Activities and Projects for Grades 4–8* published by GoodYearBooks. Copyright © 1996 Sharon Vogt.

5. What shapes are present in your daily movements? If there are no shapes in the movements drawn on these two pages, think of activities where your movements create a shape. What shapes do your movements tend to make?

_____

_____

_____

_____

From *OlympicMath: Gold Medal Activities and Projects for Grades 4–8* published by GoodYearBooks. Copyright © 1996 Sharon Vogt.

Challenge problem

6. If possible, watch a figure skating competition. Draw a portion of the movements of one of the skaters in the space above. Do modern figure skaters make figure eights? What shapes do their movements make? If you can't watch a figure skating competition, choose one sport to watch. Draw some of the shapes the players' movements make.

Favorite events

People who enjoy the Olympics usually have a favorite event. Choose several family members or friends to interview. Ask each one which Summer Olympic event he or she likes best. Then ask about Winter Olympic events. *(A list of all competitions for Summer and Winter Olympics appears on pages 94-96.)* Record their responses. Note their age and whether they are male or female. Using a record-keeping device like the one shown below may be helpful.

Age	M/F	Favorite summer event	Favorite winter event
12	F	gymnastics	skiing
16	M	soccer	bobsleds
32	F	gymnastics	figure skating
37	M	soccer	speed skating
10	M	cycling	skiing
11	M	soccer	skiing
12	F	tennis	bobsled
8	F	soccer	figure skating
9	M	basketball	bobsled
8	F	basketball	speed skating
10	F	soccer	skiing
15	M	basketball	ice hockey

Use the information in the chart you created to answer the following questions.

1. What sport is the most popular in the Summer Olympics?

_____

2. What sport do people under the age of 16 enjoy the most?

_____

From *Olympic Math: Gold Medal Activities and Projects for Grades 4-8* published by GoodYearBooks. Copyright © 1996 Sharon Vogt.

3. How many females enjoy Soccer?

_____

4. What sport do males enjoy the most?

_____

Sort your data into categories. Use the data to create two different graphs. These graphs should show completely different information. For example, one could display the favorite sports of adults while the other compares the favorite sports of boys and girls. The circle graph below shows how the males in one survey were divided in selecting their favorite Summer Olympic events.

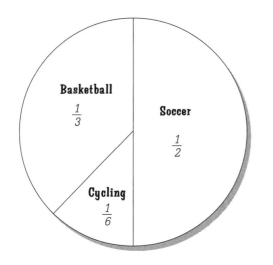

Make a circle graph using your chart and answer the following questions.

5. Which summer sport did males like the most?

_____

6. How many Winter Olympic events did the males select?

_____

7. What percent of the males selected Soccer as their favorite Summer Olympic event?

_____

8. If you had interviewed 60 males and the responses divided into the same fractions as reported in the circle graph, how many males would have chosen Cycling as their favorite Summer Olympic event? Explain how you calculated your answer.

_____

_____

9. In answering questions 4 and 5, was it easier to find the answer in the chart or the circle graph? Why?

_____

 Favorite events

Where in the world are . . . ?

Some countries always do well in certain events. Some events seem not to be dominated by one country. The graphs on the following pages show which countries have won multiple gold medals in Equestrian, Skiing, and Luge events.

Equestrian gold medal winners

Country	Number of gold medals received between 1896 and 1992
SWE	●●●●●●●●●
HOL	●●●
GER	●●●●●●●●●●●●●●
FRA	●●●●●
AUS	●●
ITA	●●●
GBR	●●●
USA	●●●●
NZE	●
SOV	●●●
SWI	●●
MEX	●

● = 2 Gold medals
BEL, CZE, JPN, POL, SPA, CAN, NLA, and AUT have each received only one gold medal during this time period.

Skiing gold medal winners

Country	Number of gold medals received between 1896 and 1992
FRA	●●●
ITA	●●●
AUT	●●●●●●
SWI	●●●●
USA	●●
SWE	●●●●●●
NOR	●●●●●●●●●
GER	●●●
FIN	●●●●●●●
SOV	●●●●●●●
GDR	●●

● = 4 Gold medals
SPA, LIE, CZE, JPN, POL, CAN, and EUN have each earned 4 or less medals.

1. Which country has earned the most gold medals in Equestrian events?

_____

2. In which sport has Austria had the most success?

_____

From OlympicMath: Gold Medal Activities and Projects for Grades 4-8 published by GoodYearBooks. Copyright © 1996 Sharon Vogt.

Luge gold medal winners

Country	Number of gold medals received between 1896 and 1992
GDR	●●●●●●●●
AUT	●
ITA	●
GER	●●
SOV	●

● = 2 Gold medals

3. Which sport(s) seem to be dominated by one country?

_____

4. Which two countries dominate the Equestrian events?

_____

_____

5. How many gold medals has the United States received in Equestrian events?

_____

6. How many more gold medals has Norway received in Skiing events than Austria?

_____

From *OlympicMath: Gold Medal Activities and Projects for Grades 4–8* published by GoodYearBooks. Copyright © 1996 Sharon Vogt.

7. Which country(ies) has achieved some success in all three sports?

_____

_____

8. In which sport has France earned more gold medals, Equestrian or Skiing? How many more gold medals has France earned in its more successful sport?

_____

9. The chart shows about the same number of symbols for Italy in Skiing events and Equestrian events. Does this mean that country won the same number of gold medals in both of these events? Why or why not?

_____

_____

10. Find a map of the world. Locate the countries with Skiing gold medals on the map. What do these countries have in common?

_____

_____

11. How does this similarity contribute to the success these countries achieve in Skiing events?

_____

_____

12. Think of the other sports in the Winter Olympics. Do you think the United States dominates any of the winter events? Explain your thinking.

_____

_____

13. Name two Olympic sports that you think the United States dominates. Explain why you chose these two sports. Use an almanac to find out if you are correct.

_____

_____

From _OlympicMath: Gold Medal Activities and Projects for Grades 4–8_ published by GoodYearBooks. Copyright © 1996 Sharon Vogt.

What does the future hold?

Ever since records of athletic accomplishment have been kept, athletes have trained harder and longer to beat them. In doing so, they constantly establish new world records that future athletes attempt to outdo.

    The charts below show the progression of world records over the years for a few Olympic events. Make one graph for each chart. Plot a point on the graph for each Olympic year. If the world record did not improve from the previous Olympic year, plot a point at the same place as the previous year. No improvements were made in 1992 in the world records for the High Jump and the 800-Meter Freestyle.

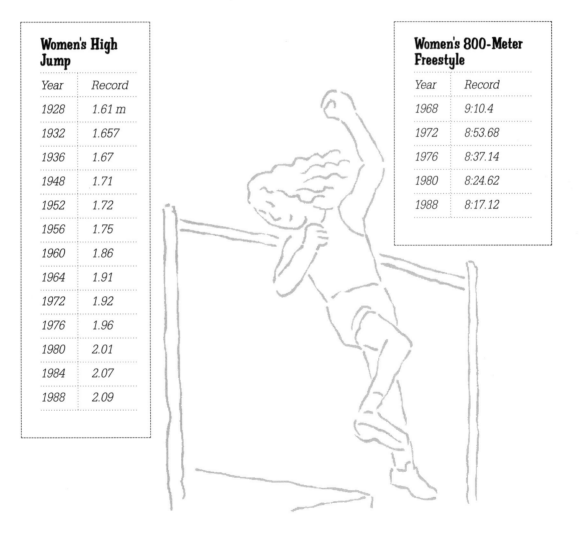

Women's High Jump

Year	Record
1928	1.61 m
1932	1.657
1936	1.67
1948	1.71
1952	1.72
1956	1.75
1960	1.86
1964	1.91
1972	1.92
1976	1.96
1980	2.01
1984	2.07
1988	2.09

Women's 800-Meter Freestyle

Year	Record
1968	9:10.4
1972	8:53.68
1976	8:37.14
1980	8:24.62
1988	8:17.12

From *OlympicMath: Gold Medal Activities and Projects for Grades 4–8* published by GoodYearBooks. Copyright © 1996 Sharon Vogt.

1.   Women's High Jump

2.   Women's 800-Meter Freestyle

Use your graphs to answer the
following questions:

3. In which sport has improvement been
the slowest?

_____

4. In which sport has improvement been
the fastest?

_____

5. In the Women's 800-Meter Freestyle,
the improvement has been less
dramatic since 1980. If improvement
continues to follow the new pattern,
in what year would you expect a
woman to swim 800 meters in under
8 seconds?

_____

Describe the patterns you see in the
improvement shown in the graphs.

6. Which sport is most likely to improve
the most in the coming years?
Explain your reasoning.

_____

_____

7. Women's High Jump

_____

8. Women's 800-Meter Freestyle

_____

From *OlympicMath: Gold Medal Activities and Projects for Grades 4–8* published by GoodYearBooks. Copyright © 1996 Sharon Vogt.

 What does the future hold?

Equipment costs

Some Olympic sports are quite costly. Many athletes must pay private coaches to ready them for competition, and some athletes must purchase expensive equipment. Use the drawings below to calculate the total cost of equipment for several Olympic sports.

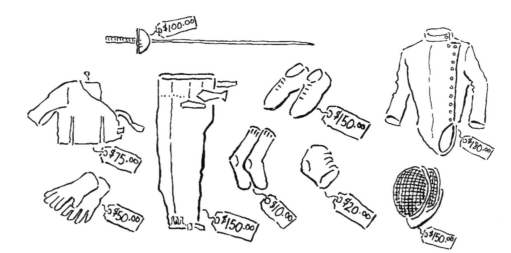

1. Sabre Fencing
The equipment above is used by athletes in the Sabre Fencing competitions. Competitors are required to bring two sabres to a competition in case one is damaged. If a competitor decides to keep four sabres to be on the safe side, how much does it cost for all the necessary equipment shown above?

_____

From *OlympicMath: Gold Medal Activities and Projects for Grades 4–8* published by GoodYearBooks. Copyright © 1996 Sharon Vogt.

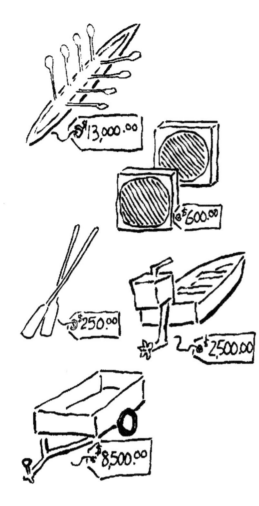

3. Figure Skating
Olympic skaters replace their skate boots about three times a year, but the blades last over one year. They also need at least two different costumes; more as they enter more competitions. How much will it cost a female skater for two costumes, skateboots, and blades for a year?

_____

2. Rowing
The equipment above is used by an eight-person rowing team. If the team shared the costs evenly, how much would each member of the team have to pay for the equipment needed?

_____

4. Choose your favorite Olympic sport. Research the costs of the equipment needed to compete. If no special equipment is required, find out how much it costs to go to preliminary competitions and pay the salary of a private coach. Describe and total your findings in the space below.

_____

_____

_____

The camera's eye

Television never covers every Olympic event in its entirety; there just isn't enough time. Program managers must decide which events the viewers enjoy most. They may televise entire competitions of the most popular events and show only highlights of the less popular events.

Consider the Olympics that will occur next. Use the circle graph below to estimate the amount of coverage you think each event will receive. Will one event dominate half of the broadcast time? Will each event receive approximately the same coverage with only a few events receiving slightly more coverage? If you were the program manager, how would you divide the available air time? Show your results in the circle graph below.

During the next Olympic broadcast, check your estimate. Use the list of Summer or Winter Olympic events at the back of this book. Look at the Olympic schedule in your television guide. Calculate the total broadcast time for each event. Use the circle on the next page to create another circle graph.

My estimate

From *OlympicMath: Gold Medal Activities and Projects for Grades 4–8* published by GoodYearBooks. Copyright © 1996 Sharon Vogt.

Actual programming

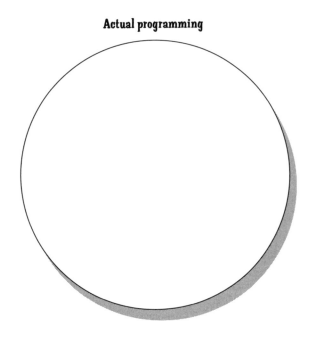

1. How does your estimate compare to this circle graph? Are there any similarities?

_____

_____

2. What are the major differences? Why do you suppose the producers decided to cover the Olympic events in this way?

_____

_____

PROJECTS

Planning an Olympic village

In the early days of the Olympics, host cities built small villages to accommodate the athletes and their competitions. In more recent years, host cities, finding construction costs to be too high, have chosen to utilize standing buildings and athletic centers. Sometimes host cities will construct one new building to commemorate the Olympics. Cities often use college facilities, such as the swimming pool, dormitories, and the track. Local arenas or stadiums are used to hold the more popular events. The chart below shows the venues (*locations*) of the 1996 Summer Olympics in and around Atlanta, Georgia. The only building constructed specifically for the Olympics was the Olympic Stadium.

Events	Location
Opening and Closing Ceremonies, Athletics	Olympic Stadium
Archery, Cycling - Track, Tennis	Stone Mountain Park
Badminton	Georgia State University
Baseball	Atlanta-Fulton County Stadium
Basketball, Gymnastics	Georgia Dome (Morehouse College)
Boxing	Alexander Memorial Coliseum
Canoe - Sprint, Rowing	Lake Lanier
Canoe - Slalom	Ocoee River
Cycling - Mountain Bike, Equestrian	Georgia International Horse Park
Cycling - Road	Streets of Atlanta
Diving, Swimming, Synchronized Swimming, Water Polo	Georgia Tech Aquatic Center
Fencing, Handball, Judo, Table Tennis, Weightlifting, Wrestling	Georgia World Congress Center
Soccer - Finals	Sanford Stadium
Hockey	Clark Atlanta University (Morris Brown College)
Shooting	Wolf Creek Shooting Complex
Softball	Golden Park
Volleyball	University of Georgia and Omni Coliseum
Yachting	Wassaw Sound

From *OlympicMath: Gold Medal Activities and Projects for Grades 4–8* published by GoodYearBooks. Copyright © 1996 Sharon Vogt.

Imagine that the Olympics are being held in your city or a nearby metropolitan area. Which Games would most likely be hosted in your area, Summer or Winter? What buildings could be used to hold the Olympic events? Make a plan for an Olympic village. Choose the Olympics *(Summer or Winter)* your city could host. On a separate sheet of paper, copy the list of Olympic events to be held. Get information about the buildings and parks in your area. Will one or more new buildings be needed? Next to each event, write the name of the building or location that is capable of holding the event. Describe the purpose, proposed name, and location of any new buildings. Sometimes the Olympics are held within several cities and planning includes transportation between the cities. When choosing locations for events, you might want to consider places in surrounding cities and states.

After you have determined the location of every Olympic event, draw a map of them. Since the map may include buildings that are several miles apart, draw your map to scale. Find the distance between the two buildings that are the farthest from each other. Determine what scale must be used to place these two buildings on the same page.

Include transportation plans on your map. You may want to plan for the construction of a new mass–transit system to accommodate travelers if many of the Olympic events will be held in places quite a few miles apart. Design a symbol to represent each method of transportation *(bus, train, subway, etc.)* and show the routes each will run. Remember to create a key and a legend to let map readers know the scale of the map and what your symbols represent.

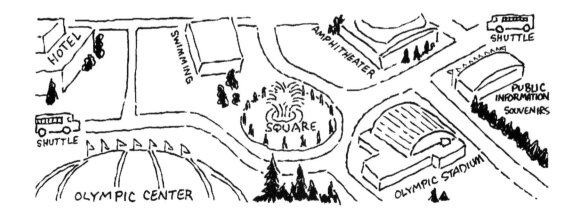

Olympic revenues

One of the major ways a host city brings in revenues is by the sale of tickets to Olympic events. The chart shown here lists the prices for tickets to 1996 Olympic events in Atlanta, Georgia.

Event	Ticket prices	Midrange ticket prices
Opening and Closing Ceremonies	$200-600	$400
Archery	$10-25	
Athletics	$20-250	
Badminton	$15-35	
Baseball	$6-60	
Basketball	$10-250	
Boxing	$25-175	
Canoe - Sprint	$10-30	
Canoe - Slalom	$10-15	
Cycling - Mountain Bike	$15	
Cycling - Road	$0	
Cycling - Track	$23-35	
Diving	$20-150	
Equestrian	$10-75	
Fencing	$10-75	
Soccer - Finals	$25-125	
Gymnastics- Artistic	$25-250	
Gymnastics - Rhythmic	$10-50	
Handball	$15-25	
Hockey	$10-25	
Judo	$20-40	
Modern Pentathlon	$25	
Rowing	$10-30	
Shooting	$20	
Softball	$15-30	
Swimming	$25-150	
Synchronized Swimming	$10-45	
Table Tennis	$10-25	
Tennis	$20-125	
Volleyball	$15-125	
Water Polo	$20-50	
Weightlifting	$20-40	
Wrestling	$20-40	

From *OlympicMath: Gold Medal Activities and Projects for Grades 4–8* published by GoodYearBooks. Copyright © 1996 Sharon Vogt.

1. Which event has the most expensive ticket?

_____

2. How many events offer some tickets less than $25?

_____

3. Calculate the midrange ticket price for each event listed. Write your answers on the chart.

4. Why do you think there are ranges of prices for each event, rather than just one ticket price?

_____

Challenge problem

5. Why do you think tickets for some events are so much more expensive than others? What makes the Swimming events cost more to attend than the Weightlifting events?

Use the plans you made in the previous section *(Planning an Olympic Village)* and the chart on the following page for this project. Estimate the revenue tickets could generate if the Olympics were held in your area. Try to find an accurate estimate of the seating capacity of each building or location you planned to use for Olympic events. If you cannot find seating capacities for some locations, use those reported for the 1984 Summer Olympics in Los Angeles, California *(found on page 6)*, as a guide.

Next, select a midrange ticket price for each event. Use the ticket prices in Atlanta as a guide. Have prices of everyday items increased or decreased since the beginning of 1996? Plan changes in ticket prices accordingly. Record all data on the chart that follows.

Finally, multiply the seating capacity by the midrange ticket price for each event to estimate the revenues for each event. Figure the sum of these individual revenues to find the total ticket revenues.

Consider the plans and estimates you made in the last two activities. Are your plans realistic? Do you think your city could actually host the Olympics? Consider sending a letter to your mayor. Describe the activities you have completed and enclose your plans and estimates. You could be the one to initiate a plan for the Olympics to come to your area.

From *OlympicMath: Gold Medal Activities and Projects for Grades 4–8* published by GoodYearBooks. Copyright © 1996 Sharon Vogt.

From *OlympicMath: Gold Medal Activities and Projects for Grades 4–8* published by GoodYearBooks. Copyright © 1996 Sharon Vogt.

Events	Seating capacity	Midrange ticket prices	Ticket revenue
Grand total:			

Competing against yourself

Athletes must prepare constantly for the Olympics; they can't wait to be invited to a national or world competition. To motivate themselves to improve, athletes will often compete against themselves. Each time they perform their sports, they try to improve their own record. Even team players may compete against themselves at some time. They often run drills that help them improve a specific skill required by their sport. Soccer players may practice directing the ball with their heads or their knees. Basketball players may practice their free–throw shots.

Below is a chart showing a basketball player's daily record in making free–throw shots. Complete the chart.

Day	Free-throw attempts	Baskets made	Percent of shots made	Percent inc/dec
1	25	10	40%	—
2	20	10	50%	25% Inc
3	30	18		
4	30	16		
5	50	30		
6	45	28		
7	30	20		
8		26	65%	
9	35		60%	
10	50			10% Inc

Choose two events or two physical skills *(like shooting free–throws)* in which you would like to improve. Record your performance for two weeks on graph paper. After the two weeks, analyze your performance. How much did you improve? When did you do the most improving? What contributed to your improvement other than the constant practice?

From *OlympicMath: Gold Medal Activities and Projects for Grades 4–8* published by GoodYearBooks. Copyright © 1996 Sharon Vogt.

Simulation table tennis

Planning a tournament requires know-how, patience, and a full understanding of how a tournament is run. In the Olympics, both individuals and teams play table tennis. This activity involves a tournament of individual players, but team competition is very similar. At the start of the tournament, players are split into groups. Each group holds its own round-robin tournament. *Round robin* simply means that each player completes a match against every other player. A *match* consists of two individuals playing a number of games until one player has won three games. After all the matches are played, the records of wins and losses are compared. The two individuals from each group having the best records continue on to an elimination tournament.

1. Since a player must win three games against each competitor, what is the most number of games that could be played against the same person?

_____

2. Ten people are entered in a table-tennis tournament and are split into two groups of equal number. How many matches must be played to determine which players go on to the elimination round?

_____

3. Describe how to determine the number of matches to be played before the elimination round. You know the number of players entered in the tournament and the number of groups into which they will be divided.

_____

_____

_____

4. On the next page is a table showing the names of table-tennis players entered in a tournament. The tournament sponsors have decided to divide the players into two groups. Organize a similar or imaginary tournament. Assign players to their separate groups. Make a list of players involved in each match. For each pairing, roll a die. If you roll an even number, the first player listed wins a game. If you roll an odd number, the second player listed wins a game. Continue rolling the die until you have a winner of the match. Keep track of the game and match wins and losses each player accumulates. Record the total number of each player's game and match wins and losses on the table.

5. What is the probability of a player winning a simulation game?

_____

From *OlympicMath: Gold Medal Activities and Projects for Grades 4–8* published by GoodYearBooks. Copyright © 1996 Sharon Vogt.

	Games			Matches			
Name	Win	Loss	W.P.	Win	Loss	W.P.	Rank
Chen Kim							
Erik Persson							
Li Jing							
Hyun Wan							
Yelena Valentina							
Jan Appelgren							
Cecelia Waldner							
Kenneth Brown							

WP = winning percentage

6. What is the probability of a player winning three simulation games in a row?

_____

7. Using your recorded data, calculate each player's winning percentage *(W.P.)*. Use the winning percentages to help you rank the players within their separate groups from 1 to 4 with a rank of 1 given to the best player in each group.

8. The top two players in each group continue on to an elimination round. In our competition, they play each other in one match. The loser is eliminated while the winner continues by playing the winner of the other match. Above is a diagram for an elimination round. Begin by listing the winners from the round-robin competitions on the lines in the first column. The first two players listed play each other as do the second pair listed. Use your die to decide who wins each match in the semifinals as you did in the round robin. Write the winners of these two games in the second column. These two winners play each other in the finals. Use your die again to determine the winner and write his or her name in the last column.

Semifinals   *Finals*   *Winner*

_____

_____

_____

_____

From *OlympicMath: Gold Medal Activities and Projects for Grades 4–8* published by GoodYearBooks. Copyright © 1996 Sharon Vogt.

From *OlympicMath: Gold Medal Activities and Projects for Grades 4–8* published by GoodYearBooks. Copyright © 1996 Sharon Vogt.

9. Consider elimination rounds for other numbers of players. What multiples work best in this format?

_____

10. How many matches would have to be played during the elimination round if eight players qualified?

_____

11. Look at the number of matches played when even more players compete. Describe a situation that causes an even number of matches to be played.

_____

Challenge problem

12. If a player lost a match in the fourth round of play during an elimination round, what is the least number of players that could be competing?

_____

Fantasy Olympic team

You can create your own fantasy Olympic team and compete against other fantasy teams. Choose your favorite nonteam Olympic sport. Research statistics on current or recent athletes in this sport. These statistics should include their scores in several competitions. Try to locate scores for six different competitions. You may be able to find these statistics in sporting magazines or books. You can also write to the governing body of the sport, which may have the statistics you are looking for, or can point you in the right direction. If you are unable to find this data for your favorite sport, consider your second favorite sport. Organize your data on the chart below.

Athlete	Recent scores, win/loss ratios, or rankings					

How many athletes does your sport send to the Olympics? Using the statistics you found, choose the athletes you would send to represent the United States. Draw a star next to the names of the people on the chart who will be on your team.

From *OlympicMath: Gold Medal Activities and Projects for Grades 4–8* published by GoodYearBooks. Copyright © 1996 Sharon Vogt.

Now that you have assembled your team, it is time to compete. If another student in your class has chosen the same sport, your teams can compete. Designate one team as USA1 and the other as USA2. Or you can create your own imaginary teams from other countries. Use the athletes you didn't choose for your own team to create teams for at least two other countries.

On the chart that follows, list *all* the athletes competing, both your team members and their opponents. Note the country for which they are competing in the second column. Roll a die and write the result in the third column. Each athlete receives one roll of the die. After recording the result, consult your statistical chart. If you rolled a one, the athlete scores the same as the first score reported on the chart. If you rolled a two, the athlete receives the second score from the chart, and so on. Write the assigned score in the fourth column of the chart. If you found less than six scores for each athlete, decide what you will do when you roll a number for which you do not have a score.

Once all the scores are in, rank the athletes as to who performed the best. Then answer the following questions:

1. Which team's players had the best scores overall going into the competition?

_____

2. Which team performed the best during the competition?

_____

From *OlympicMath: Gold Medal Activities and Projects for Grades 4–8* published by GoodYearBooks. Copyright © 1996 Sharon Vogt.

Athlete	Country	Roll of the die	Score	Rank

3. Which player had earned the highest score before the competition?

_____

4. Which player earned the highest score during the competition?

_____

5. Do you think the results of your simulated competition are realistic? If the athletes competed in real life, do you think the results could be similar to your simulation? Explain your thinking.

_____

_____

_____

From *OlympicMath: Gold Medal Activities and Projects for Grades 4–8* published by GoodYearBooks. Copyright © 1996 Sharon Vogt.

Funding the Olympics

In another activity, you made plans for hosting the Olympics in your area. You considered the revenues ticket sales could provide. Besides the building costs, what other expenses might a host city face in putting on the Olympics? What other revenues might it earn?

Think about all that happens during the Olympics. Are new jobs available? What kinds of jobs are created? Atlanta estimates selling two million tickets for Olympic events. What might it be like for your city to grow in population by nearly a million people overnight? What additional resources might your city need?

Use this chart to record all the additional expenses and revenues the Olympics could bring to your city. Discuss your list with a friend. Help each other come up with even more ideas.

From OlympicMath: Gold Medal Activities and Projects for Grades 4–8 published by GoodYearBooks. Copyright © 1996 Sharon Vogt.

Expenses	Revenue

1. Imagine being the mayor of your city. Describe why you wouldn't want your city to host the Olympic Games.

_____

_____

2. Now describe why you, as mayor, would want your city to host the Olympic Games. What benefits, other than revenues, might the Olympics bring to your city?

_____

_____

_____

_____

From *OlympicMath: Gold Medal Activities and Projects for Grades 4–8* published by GoodYearBooks. Copyright © 1996 Sharon Vogt.

This graph shows another source of revenue for the host city. The Olympic Committee sells television stations the rights to broadcast the Games. Since only one network in the United States can purchase these rights, the networks bid for them. The one willing to pay the most money is granted the broadcasting rights.

Summer Olympics

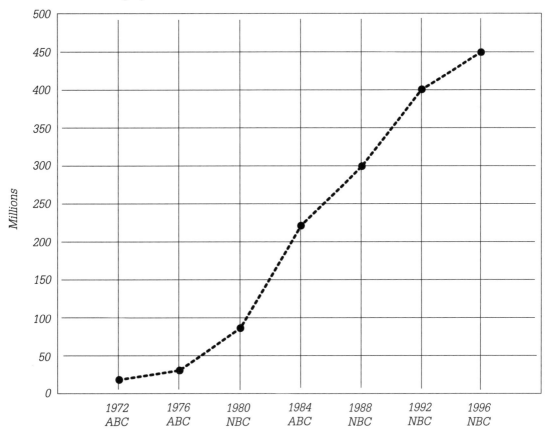

From *OlympicMath: Gold Medal Activities and Projects for Grades 4–8* published by GoodYearBooks. Copyright © 1996 Sharon Vogt.

The Olympic Committee also sells broadcasting rights to
networks in other countries. The price is usually based on how
much the country can afford. In 1984, European and Japanese
television networks paid $20 million each, while African networks
paid only $200,000.

3. Is it fair for other countries to pay less
for television broadcasting rights? What
are the benefits of this type of system?

_____

_____

4. Some businesses charge their
customers based on their ability to
pay. Which businesses do you think
should use this system? Why?

_____

_____

From *OlympicMath: Gold Medal Activities and Projects for Grades 4–8* published by GoodYearBooks. Copyright © 1996 Sharon Vogt.

How can television stations afford to pay for broadcasting rights? They sell commercials. In 1984, ABC expected to sell 2,000 commercials to bring in $600 million. A 30-second, prime-time spot cost $250,000.

5. What was the average price for a commercial during the 1984 Olympic Games?

_____

6. How much did it cost per second for a 30-second prime-time commercial?

_____

7. If the average commercial was shown during prime time, how many seconds did it run?

_____

8. ABC scheduled 12 minutes of commercials every hour. The network carried 187.5 hours of coverage of the Olympic Games. How many minutes of commercials were shown throughout the entire broadcast?

_____

9. Considering the increasing cost of broadcasting rights reflected on the graph, how much do you think a 30-minute, prime-time commercial cost during the 1996 Olympics? Describe how you calculated your answer.

_____

_____

Speed experiment

Many Olympic events require speed. Three Winter Olympic events depend on *downhill* speed. In the Bobsled, Luge, and Alpine Skiing competitions, athletes try to reach the bottom of the hill as fast as possible without putting their lives in danger. Over the years, athletes have called upon mathematicians, computer scientists, engineers, and doctors to learn more about speed. How can these people help an athlete improve his or her speed? Shouldn't the athletes be more concerned about being physically fit?

Athletes can do only so much to improve their bodies for competition. There is a limit to how strong one can become. Other changeable factors besides strength and agility can influence the competition. This activity will help you discover these changeable factors. Think about outside forces that affect how fast you can go. What can keep a car or plane from moving with unlimited speed? Have you ever slid down a hill of snow or a slippery slide? What made you go faster? What slowed you down?

On the chart that follows, make a list of factors that you think may affect speed. List them in the first column. Remember, right now you are only guessing. The factors you list are simply things you think *might* have an effect on speed. After you have conducted this experiment, you will know for certain. That's what experiments are for. They help us test ideas and clarify our thinking.

From *OlympicMath: Gold Medal Activities and Projects for Grades 4–8* published by GoodYearBooks. Copyright © 1996 Sharon Vogt.

 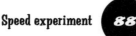

Experiment notes

Hypothesis *Speed effects*	*Experiment notes*	*Effect +/-/none*

The next step is to devise experiments to test each factor you listed on the chart. You will need to gather a few items. To test downhill speed, you need an inclined plane. An *inclined plane* is a surface that slants. You could use a nearby hill or a slide or a wooden board leaned against another surface. Next you will need something that can slide or roll down your inclined plane. If it has snowed, you could conduct your experiment on a hillside with a sled. Or, use a toy car on the slide or the wooden board. You will also need a stopwatch.

Think of how you can test your factors. Let's say one of the factors you listed is *weight*. The weight of an object may have some effect on its speed. To test this you need to change the weight of the object you are working with. First, send your object down the inclined plane by itself. Record the amount of time it took from start to finish. Next, change the weight of your object by taping a coin, wooden block, or some other object to it. Send it down the inclined plane once again timing it as it goes. Describe your experiment in the middle column of the chart. Record the two times for the object with and without additional weight.

A good scientist never draws a conclusion from only one test. Add more weight and send the object down the inclined plane once more noting its completion time on the chart. Compare the times. Did the time increase or decrease as more weight was added?

In the third column, note the effect of weight on your object. If the item got to the bottom of the inclined plane in less time with more weight, weight had a positive effect. Write a plus sign *(+)* in the third column. If it required more time for the weighted item to get to the bottom of the inclined plane, weight had a negative effect. Write a minus sign *(-)* in the third column. If the time did not change at all, weight had no effect on the speed of the item. Write "none" in the third column.

Devise experiments testing each factor you listed in the first column of the chart. Remember to test each factor at least twice. If there seems to be no effect or the time change is very small, you should change the factor one more time to be sure.

From *OlympicMath: Gold Medal Activities and Projects for Grades 4–8* published by GoodYearBooks. Copyright © 1996 Sharon Vogt.

Planning a trip to the Olympics

Imagine you and your family are planning a vacation to the next Summer or Winter Olympics. When and where are the next Summer and Winter Olympics? Which one would you like to see? Choose one and plan a vacation for your family.

Find out more information about the place where the Olympics are being held. How far will you have to travel? Where will you stay? How many days will you want to stay? Are there other sites you would like to see while you are there? Use the following as a guide to organize your planning.

Transportation

Number of miles from your home to the city where the Olympics will be held:

_____

Transportation options	Time required for one-way travel	Prices for adults and children	Total cost
Plane			
Train			
Bus			
Car			
Other			

From OlympicMath: Gold Medal Activities and Projects for Grades 4–8 published by GoodYearBooks. Copyright © 1996 Sharon Vogt.

Hotel Accommodations

Locate three hotels in or around the Olympic village. Write "yes" in the third column if the hotel will run a shuttle bus. If you will have to provide your own transportation during your stay, calculate the cost of renting a car.

Hotel	Miles from Olympic Village	Transportation?	Cost per night	Total cost

Food, tickets, and other expenses

What other expenses can you expect during your vacation? Use the estimates you made earlier for ticket prices to Olympic events. You will probably eat in restaurants during most of your stay. What is the cost of an average meal? What other sites would you like to visit? Do they charge an admission fee? On the table here, create a list of expenses and the total amount each activity will cost your family.

Item	Cost

From OlympicMath: Gold Medal Activities and Projects for Grades 4–8 published by GoodYearBooks. Copyright © 1996 Sharon Vogt.

Options

On the table below, make three different Olympic vacation plans. You have assembled costs for several different modes of transportation, three hotels, and a wide variety of possible expenses. You have many choices. Make different choices for each plan. You may want to make one plan that includes everything. This could be your ultimate dream vacation. Another plan could be more moderately priced, and the last designed for vacationers on a tight budget. List your choices and their prices. Calculate a total price for each separate plan.

Plan #1	Plan #2	Plan #3
Total		

Olympic events

Summary Games

Archery

Badminton

Baseball

Basketball

Boxing

Canoeing
    Kayak
    Canadian
    Kayak Slalom
    Canadian Slalom

Cycling
    1,000 to 4,000–Meter races
    50–Kilometer points race
    Road race

Equestrian
    Three-day Event
    Jumping
    Dressage

Fencing
    Foil
    Epée
    Sabre

Field Hockey

Football *(soccer)*

Gymastics
    All-Around
    Horizontal Bar
    Parallel Bars
    Long Horse Vault
    Side Horse *(pommeled horse)*
    Rings
    Floor Exercises
    Team Combined Exercises
    Asymmetrical *(uneven)* Bars
    Balance Beam
    Rhythmic All-Around

Handball

Judo

Modern Pentathlon

Rowing
    Sculls
    Oared Shell with and without coxswain

Shooting
    Rapid-fire pistol
    Free pistol
    Air pistol
    Small-bore rifle, prone
    Small-bore rifle, three positions
    Air rifle
    Moving target
    Sport pistol
    Trap shooting
    Skeet shooting

Swimming
  Freestyle
  Backstroke
  Breaststroke
  Butterfly
  Individual Medley
  Freestyle Relay
  Medley Relay
  Springboard Diving
  Platform Diving
  Water Polo
  Synchronized Swimming

Table Tennis

Tennis

Track and Field
  100–10,000 Meter races
  Marathon
  Hurdles
  Steeplechase
  Relay
  Walk
  High Jump
  Pole Vault
  Long Jump
  Triple Jump
  Shot Put
  Discus Throw
  Hammer Throw
  Javelin Throw
  Decathlon
  Heptathlon
  Volleyball

Weightlifting

Wrestling, freestyle

Wrestling, greco-roman

Yachting
  Boardsailing
  Finn
  470
  Europe
  Star
  Flying Dutchman
  Tornado
  Soling

Olympic events

Winter Games

Biathlon
    7.5–20 Kilometers Relay

Bobsled

Ice hockey

Luge *(toboggan)*

Skating, figure
    Single
    Pairs
    Ice Dance

Skating, speed
    500 to 10,000–Meter races
    Short Track
    Short Track Relay

Skiing, Alpine
    Downhill
    Slalom
    Alpine Combined

Skiing, Freestyle

Skiing, nordic
    15–50 Kilometers
    Combined Pursuit
    Relay
    Ski Jump
    Nordic Combined

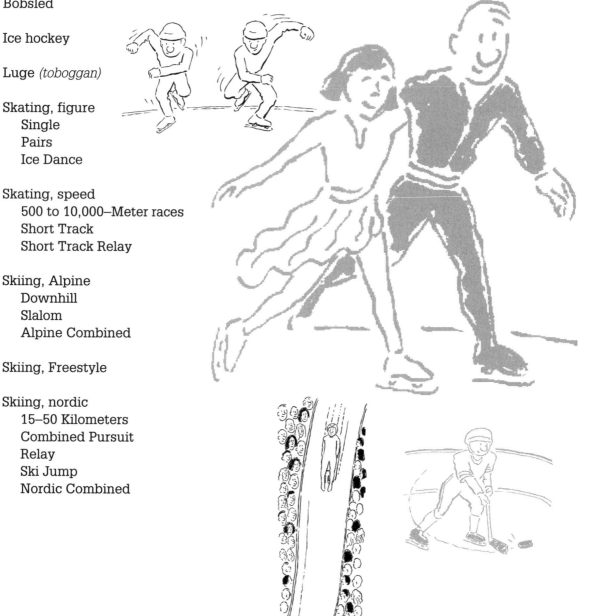

Nation abbreviations

AFG	Afghanistan		CHA	Chad
AHO	Netherlands Antilles		CHI	Chile
ALB	Albania		CHN	China
ALG	Algeria		CIV	Ivory Coast
AND	Andorra		CMR	Cameroon
ANG	Angola		COK	Cook Islands
ANT	Antigua		COL	Colombia
ARG	Argentina		CRC	Costa Rica
ARM	Armenia		CRO	Croatia
ARU	Aruba		CUB	Cuba
ASA	American Samoa		CYP	Cyprus
AUS	Australia		DEN	Denmark
AUT	Austria		DJI	Djibouti
AZE	Azerbaijan		DOM	Dominican Republic
BAH	Bahamas		ECU	Ecuador
BAN	Bangladesh		EGY	Egypt
BAR	Barbados		ESA	El Salvador
BEL	Belgium		ESP	Spain
BEN	Benin		EST	Estonia
BER	Bermuda		ETH	Ethiopia
BHU	Bhutan		FIJ	Fiji
BIZ	Belize		FIN	Finland
BLS	Belarus		FRA	France
BOL	Bolivia		GAB	Gabon
BOT	Botswana		GAM	Gambia
BRA	Brazil			
BRN	Bahrain			
BRU	Brunei			
BSH	Bosnia Herzegovina			
BUL	Bulgaria			
BUR	Burkina Faso			
CAF	Central African Republic			
CAN	Canada			
CAY	Cayman Islands			
CGO	Congo			

GBR	Great Britain and Northern Ireland	LBR	Liberia
GEO	Georgia	LIE	Liechtenstein
GEQ	Equitorial Guinea	LIT	Lithuania
GER	Germany	LUX	Luxembourg
GHA	Ghana	MAD	Madagascar
GRE	Greece	MEX	Mexico
GRN	Grenada	MGL	Mongolia
GUA	Guatemala	MAR	Morocco
GUI	Guinea	MAS	Malaysia
GUM	Guam	MAW	Malawi
GUY	Guyana	MDV	Maldives
HAI	Haiti	MLD	Moldova
HKG	Hong Kong	MLI	Mali
HON	Honduras	MLT	Malta
HUN	Hungary	MON	Monaco
INA	Indonesia	MOZ	Mozambique
IND	India	MRI	Mauritius
IRI	Islamic Republic of Iran	MTN	Mauritania
IRL	Ireland *(Eire)*	MYA	Union of Myanmar *(formerly Burma)*
IRQ	Iraq		
ISL	Iceland	NAM	Namibia
ISR	Israel	NCA	Nicaragua
ISV	Virgin Islands	NED	The Netherlands
ITA	Italy	NEP	Nepal
IVB	British Virgin Islands	NGR	Nigeria
JAM	Jamaica	NIG	Niger
JOR	Jordan	NOR	Norway
JPN	Japan	NZL	New Zealand
KEN	Kenya	OMA	Oman
KGZ	Kyrgyzstan	PAK	Pakistan
KOR	Korea *(South)*		
KSA	Kingdom of Saudi Arabia		
KUW	Kuwait		
KZK	Kazakhstan		
LAO	Laos		
LAT	Latvia		
LES	Lesotho		
LIB	Lebanon		
LBA	Libya		

PAN	Panama	TRI	Trinidad and Tobago
PAR	Paraguay	TUN	Tunisia
PER	Peru	TUR	Turkey
PHI	Philippines	UAE	United Arab Emirates
PNG	Papua-New Guinea	UGA	Uganda
POL	Poland	UKR	Ukraine
POR	Portugal	URU	Uruguay
PRK	Democratic People's Republic of Korea (North)	USA	United States of America
		UZB	Uzbekistan
PUR	Puerto Rico	VAN	Vanuatu
QAT	Qatar	VEN	Venezuela
ROM	Romania	VIE	Vietnam
RSA	Republic of South Africa	VIN	St. Vincent and the Grenadines
RUS	Russia	YEM	Yemen
RWA	Rwanda	YUG	Yugoslavia
SAM	Western Samoa	ZAI	Zaire
SEN	Senegal	ZAM	Zambia
SEY	Seychelles	ZIM	Zimbabwe
SIN	Singapore		
SLE	Sierra Leone		
SLO	Slovenia		

Other abbreviations used in activities:

SMR	San Marino	CAM	Cameroon
SOL	Solomon Islands	CZE	Czechoslovakia
SOM	Somalia	GDR	East Germany (used 1956–1988)
SRI	Sri Lanka	ICE	Iceland
SUD	Sudan	IVC	Ivory Coast
SUI	Switzerland	LEB	Lebanon
SUR	Surinam	MOR	Morocco
SVK	Slovakia	NZE	New Zealand
SWE	Sweden	SOV	Soviet Union
SWZ	Swaziland	SPA	Spain
SYR	Syria	SWI	Switzerland
TAN	Tanzania		
TCH	Czech Republic		
TGA	Tonga		
THA	Thailand		
TJK	Tajikistan		
TKM	Turkmenistan		
TOG	Togo		
TPE	Chinese Taipei		

Answer key

Olympic riddles
1. Ralph Jefferson
2. Eva Bevin
3. Ingrid Schafer and Rita Hoff
4. Brigit Mageste and Rob Robertson
5. Peitro Mendez
6. Suzanna Haven
7. Carlton Peige
8. Joseph Spekinski

Olympic sites
1. 7
2. France and the United States have both hosted three Winter Olympics.
3. United States
4. 10
5. Places must have conditions appropriate for the events to be held. There is no place in Houston, Texas, to hold the events that require snow.
6. Answers will vary.
7. Answers will vary.

Spectators
1. Athletics, Basketball, Handball, Volleyball, and Wrestling
2. thousands place
3. Athletics–93,000; Basketball–18,000; Handball–18,000; Volleyball–11,000; Wrestling–9,000
4. Football
5. hundred thousands
6. 24,000
7. The value of the 4 in the seating capacity for Equestrian events is ten times more than the value of the other 4.
8. Field Hockey
9. 264,000
10. No, there were 837,000 tickets for the Athletics events.
11. thousands

Medal-winning countries
1. United States
2. Soviet Union
3. United States
4. Soviet Union
5. 6
6. In 1980, 36 countries received medals and in 1984, 47 countries received medals.
7. More countries received medals in 1984 than in 1980.
8. The change could be due to the increased number of countries that participate in the Olympics.
9. The same number of gold medals were awarded in 1980 as in 1984.
10. The only thing that would change the number of gold medals awarded is an increase or reduction in the number of events.
11. More countries earned 20 or less medals.
12. With the large number of countries that participate in the Olympics, it will probably always be true that more countries earn 20 or less medals than earn more than 20. Many of the smaller countries may not even enter 20 people in the Olympic Games.

Medal-winning greats
1. 0.43 second
2. 1.78 seconds
3. 20 years
4. In 1964 , she jumped 2 inches higher than her 1960 jump.
5. 79.275
   Challenge problems
6. Wyomia would win both times, the first with a time of 9.8 and again with a time of 9.48.
7. 8.55 meters per second = 30,780 meters per hour = 3.08 kilometers per hour

Training goals
1. 90 days
2. In just under 9 minutes
3. 23 seconds
4. January 20
   The following goals should be noted on the calendar:
   January 12–100 meters–28 seconds
   January 17–1 mile–9:40
   January 20–1 mile–9:36
   January 22–100 meters–27 seconds
   February 1–1 mile–9:20–100 Meters–26 seconds
   February 7–1 mile–9:12

From *OlympicMath: Gold Medal Activities and Projects for Grades 4–8* published by GoodYearBooks. Copyright © 1996 Sharon Vogt.

February 11–100 meters–25 seconds
February 16–1 mile–9:00
February 21–100 meters–24 seconds
February 25–1 mile–8:48
March 3–1 mile–8:40–100 meters–23 seconds
March 13–100 meters–22 seconds
March 15–1 mile–8:24
March 18–1 mile–8:20
March 23–100 meters– 21 seconds

Scheduling
1. March 3, March 15, and March 30
2. 6
3. March 12
4. 4

Challenge problems
5. Kevin can lift weights every other day. Every third time, or every six days, he will lift weights with Paula.
6. The following reminders should be noted on the days specified.
   Lift weights:

   January 6, 11, 16, 21, 26, 31
   February 5, 10, 15, 20, 25
   March 2, 7, 12, 17, 22, 27

   Stairs:

   6 January 5, 9
   7 January 13, 17
   8 January 21, 25
   9 January 29, February 2
   10 February 6, 10
   11 February 14, 18
   12 February 22, 26
   13 March 2, 6
   14 March 10, 14
   15 March 18, 22
   16 March 26, 30

   100 meters:

   January 5, 8, 11, 14, 17, 20, 23, 26, 29
   February 1, 4, 7, 10, 13, 16, 19, 22, 25, 28
   March 3, 6, 9, 12, 15, 18, 21, 24, 27, 30

Gymnastics
Men's competition total scores: 118.625, 118.625, 118.85, 118.525, 118.15, 117.75, 118.225, 117.95, 113.8, 114.2

Women's competition total scores: 79.075, 79.125, 78.525, 78.774, 77.725, 79.075, 79.536, 79.299, 76, 78.675
1. Koji Kaji, Ken Gaylord, Vlad Titov, Tong Ning, Xu Fei, Louis Bonvi (Ning and Fei are tied at fourth place.)
2. Ma Yongyan, Emilia Pauca, Steffi Kerst, Olga Janz, Julie McNim, Nadia Szabo (Pauca, Kerst, and Janz are tied at second place.)
3. Men's team competition: Japan–119.125; China–119; USA–118.9; Women's team competition: USA–79.56; Hungary–79.299; Romania–79.35

Nordic skiing great
In 1956, Sixten won silver medals in the 15-kilometer and 30-kilometer races. He won a gold in the 50-kilometer and a bronze in the relay. In 1960, Sixten won a silver in the 15-kilometer and a gold in the 30-kilometer. In 1964, Sixten won a bronze in the 15-kilometer and gold medals in the 50-kilometer and relay races.

Running events
1. 100 meters
2. 1,500 meters
3. 10 kilometers
4. 11,000 centimeters
5. 1.6 kilometers
6. 500 decimeters
7. 211 dodecameters
8. 2.8 hectometers
9. Lines should measure 1 centimeter, 2 centimeters, 4 centimeters, 8 centimeters, 15 centimeters, 1.1 centimeters, 4 centimeters, 16 centimeters, and 2.8 centimeters.
10. Lines should measure 3 centimeters, 5 centimeters, 10 centimeters, and 2.11 centimeters.

How long?
1. the school building
2. distance from home to school
3. the car
4. 26 miles
   Challenge problem
5. Answers will vary.

From *OlympicMath: Gold Medal Activities and Projects for Grades 4–8* published by GoodYearBooks. Copyright © 1996 Sharon Vogt.

Using a stopwatch

1. 1:53.6
2. 2:04.03
3. 0.34 seconds
4. 1.71 seconds
5. 33.57 seconds
6. 27.41 seconds
7. 3:46.2
   Challenge problem
8. 1:58.64

Tracking track events

1. Gwen Torrence, Grace Jackson Small, Carlette Guidry, and Merlene Ottey
2. Gwen Torrence's average time was 22.1.
3. 0.7 seconds
4. 0.263 seconds
5. Katrin Doerre and M. Machado would have tied for first.
6. 1:18 or 1 minute 18 seconds
7. 56:29 or 56 minutes and 29 seconds
   Challenge problems
8. 16.26 kph and 16.61 kph
9. 2:39:07

Who won?

1. Gold–Team 16; Silver–Team 14; Bronze–Team 8 and Team 4
2. Gold–Kym; Silver–Madaline; Bronze–Tom
3. Gold–John; Silver–Sue; Bronze–Peter
4. Gold–Team 4; Silver–Team 1; Bronze–Team 2
   Challenge problem
5. Gold–Todd; Silver–Maxine; Bronze–José

The volleyball court

Students' drawings will vary. If they use the scale suggested, the diagram and its markings should have the following measurements:
Court Width–2 inches, Length–4 .
Center line–2 inches from each of the back lines.
Net length–2-2/15 inches or about 2 1/8 inches.
Width–1/5 inches or about 1/4 inches.
   Height, men–8/15 inches or about 1/2 inches.
   Height, women–59/120 inches or about 1/2 inches
Spike line–2/3 inches or about 5/8 inches
   from the centerline on either side of the net

Archery

1. and 2. There are many answers possible. Here is a list of four of the possible combinations. 1-10 and 4-5; 1-10, 1-9, 2-5, and 1-1; 1-10, 1-8, 2-5, and 1-2; 1-10, 1-7, 1-6, 1-4, and 1-3
3. 8 points
4. 3 points

Speed skating

1. In competitions involving heats, athletes have to race more than once. Depending on the time between the races, the athletes may not have as much energy the second time as the first. Also, when five or six skaters compete at once as compared to only two, there is less space on the ice for each athlete. This may force a skater to use a less familiar stride.
2. Cycling
3. Kayak Fours
4. To the nearest hundredth of a second
5. ± 0.0005 second
6. Teams
7. Answers will vary. Students may mention the fact that more people can produce more power.
8. Answers will vary. Students may realize that some events have very close finishes. The faster the racers, the greater the chance that the differences between their times will be very small and close enough to require an extremely precise timing device.
   Challenge problem
9. 55.8 kilometers per hour

Basketball

1. 152
2. 68.8%
3. Soviet Union
4. 12 teams
5. 30 games
6. 76
7. Bar, line, and pictographs would all be appropriate graphs on which to display the given data.
8. Accept any logical reason. The low scores were actually caused by the game being played outside on a playing surface that was wet from recent rains. The low number of games is only due to the fact that fewer countries entered the competition in its first year.
   Challenge problem
9. 1960

Prefix power

1. 10
2. 7
3. 5
4. 2
5. 8
6. 4
7. 6
8. 9
9. octagon
10. hexagon
11. quadrilateral
12. pentagon
13. heptagon
    Challenge problem
14. nonagon

Scoring the Decathlon

1. 800 points
2. 7.90 meters
3. About 700 points
4. About 3 minutes 51 seconds
5. 956.2 points
6. 12.5%
7. 4 minutes 2.0 seconds
8. 24.6%9. 8,000 points, 3rd place
10. 7,200 points, 6th place
11. 8,200 points, 2nd place
12. 8,600 points, 1st place
13. 7,600 points, 5th place
14. 7,800 points, 4th place

Decathlon results

1.

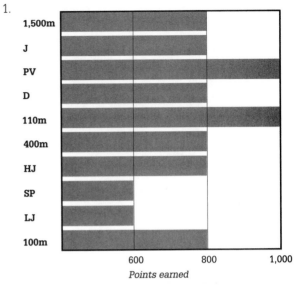

2. This graph shows that Todd's scores are only extremely low in two events—the long jump and the shot put. His best events are the hurdles and the pole vault. If he works on his running, he could bring his scores up to 1,000 in three events.

3.

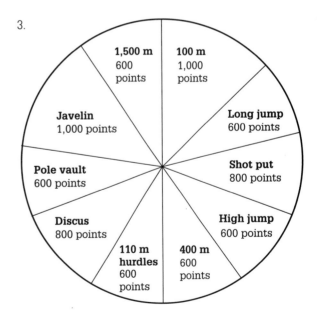

4. With this graph, Katie can see that most of her scores are 600 points. She needs improvement in all events except the 100 Meters and the Javelin. Since she does so well in the shorter running race, she may need to work on endurance.
5. If Bobby makes a double-bar graph, he can compare his performance to Christina's event by event. He will see exactly where he needs to improve and where Christina's weakness lies.

Playing coverage
1. 840 square feet; 84 square feet
2. 800 square meters; 133-1/3 square meters
3. 6,000 square yards; 600 square yards
4. 600 square meters; 100 square meters
5. 162 square meters; 27 square meters
6. 4,700 square feet; 940 square feet

Skating patterns
Answers will vary on all questions. Students will most likely recognize various forms of circles and rectangles in some of their movements.

Favorite events
Answers to all of the questions will vary.

Where in the world are . . . ?
1. Germany
2. Skiing
3. Luge
4. Germany and Sweden
5. 7
6. 14
7. Italy, Germany, and the Soviet Union
8. Skiing; 3
9. Italy received four more gold medals in Skiing events than in Equestrian events. The symbol used in the Skiing pictograph represents four gold medals. The symbol used in the Equestrian pictograph represents only two gold medals.
10. All the countries are in the middle to upper Northern Hemisphere where they are more likely to receive snow.

11. For skiers to be successful, they must live in an area where they receive a lot of snow so they have as much time as possible to practice their sport.
12. If the United States dominates in any winter sports, it would have to be one of the Skating events or Ice Hockey. The other events require snow and/or mountainous terrain which are not available in the majority of states.
13. Answers will vary. Accept all reasonable responses.

From *OlympicMath: Gold Medal Activities and Projects for Grades 4–8* published by GoodYearBooks. Copyright © 1996 Sharon Vogt.

What does the future hold?

1.

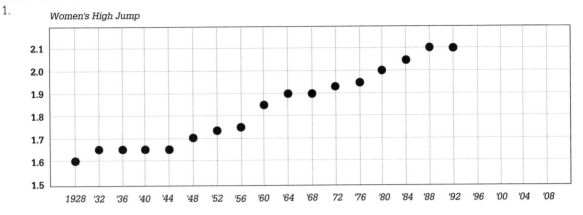

Women's High Jump

2.

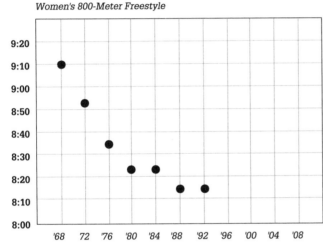

Women's 800-Meter Freestyle

3. Women's High Jump
4. Women's 800-Meter Freestyle
5. 2004
6. Since women have been competing in the 800-Meter Freestyle for only a few years, this Olympic event has a good chance for greater improvement than the other two events.
7. This record seems to be improving in a stair-step manner. The graph shows large increases followed by little or no change for the next few years.
8. The Women's 800-Meter Freestyle record improved dramatically for its first three Olympic years. Since 1980 the improvement has slowed down quite a bit.

Equipment costs
1. $3,200
2. $1,375
3. $6,900
4. Answers will vary.

The camera's eye
Answers will vary.

Planning an Olympic village
Answers will vary.

Olympic revenues
1. Opening and Closing Ceremonies
2. 28
3. Average ticket prices
   $400
   $17.50
   $135
   $25
   $33
   $130
   $100
   $20
   $12.50
   $7.50
   $0
   $29
   $85
   $42.50
   $42.50
   $75
   $137.50
   $30

$20
$17.50
$30
$12.50
$20
$20
$22.50
$87.50
27.50
$17.50
$72.50
$70
$35
$30
$30

4. The ranges in prices may reflect various levels of competition (e.g., 1st round, 2nd round, semifinals, finals), or the more expensive seats may be closer to the action than the less expensive ones.
Challenge problem
5. The more popular events may cost more than the less popular ones. Also, since seating is limited, tickets may cost more in places where less seating is available.

Competing against yourself

3. 60%; 20% increase
4. 53.3%; 11.2% decrease
5. 60%; 12.6% increase
6. 62.2%; 3.7% increase
7. 66.7%; 7.2% increase
8. 40; 2.5% decrease
9. 21; 7.7% decrease
10. 33; 66%

Simulation table tennis

1. 5
2. 20
3. Divide the total number of competitors by the number of groups. The result is the number of players in each group. Multiply the result by the next smaller whole number. This result is the number of matches each group will play. Finally, multiply by the number of groups to find the total number of matches played.
5. 1/2
6. 1/8

7. and 8. Answers will vary.
9. 7
10. multiples of 2
11. When the number of players competing is a multiple of 8, an even number of matches are played.
Challenge problem
12. 12

Fantasy team
Answers will vary.

Funding the Olympics
Some of the income and revenue possibilities your students may think of are listed below. Answers will vary. New jobs the Olympics would generate include event organizers, ticket salespeople, souvenir vendors, janitorial service providers, judges and referees, construction workers, extra health-care providers, and so on.

Expenses: printing, advertising, transportation, office expenses, more city employees, such as police officers

Revenue: taxes, broadcasting rights, sponsorship of the Games by businesses, ticket and souvenir sales, and other visitor spending

1. Hosting the Olympics requires a lot of planning and expenditures before any money begins to come in. It also requires the hiring of over a million employees for a short term. A city must have enough back-up funding and have the ability to handle large crowds. If countries decide to boycott the Olympics, it is very possible that a host city will lose money.
2. The host city receives much worldwide attention. As a result of hosting the Olympics, the city will become a tourist attraction for many years to come. People will want to visit the place they saw so much of on television.
3. and 4. Answers will vary.
5. $300,000
6. $8,333.33
7. 36 seconds
8. 2,250 minutes or 37.5 hours
9. The cost of broadcasting rights in 1996 has nearly doubled since 1984. So the cost for a 30-second, prime-time commercial probably also doubled to $500,000.

From *OlympicMath: Gold Medal Activities and Projects for Grades 4–8* published by GoodYearBooks. Copyright © 1996 Sharon Vogt.